# The Power

By

Glenn Wolkoff

May all mankind remember, understand, and accept the divinity of their origin. Set forth and observe the Universe with deliberate thought and bring form to the field of energy that connects all of us to each other and to everything else.

# The Power
By
Glenn Wolkoff

Vitae Mind Publishing
C/o Glenn Wolkoff
4804 Laurel Canyon Blvd., #190
Valley Village, CA 91607
www.vitaemind.com

Drawn by Michael Maier in 1618

# Preface

There was a sudden explosion, and the peaceful Universe I had once known was in utter chaos….shaking, movement, lights, and sounds. My underdeveloped body struggled for life against these unknown forces invading my Universe. What seemed terrifying to me was soon to become the Universe I would know.

I had no recollection of this experience from the past, even though I had been through it many times. I found myself surrounded by strangers who were touching me, grabbing me, and making scary faces and strange sounds at me.

Finally, an overwhelming feeling of loneliness set in, a feeling I was not familiar with, and one I did not care for.

So begins my incarnation, my journey as a seeker of truth; about myself, life, and the Universe around me.

# Introduction

I want to reveal to you a natural power you have that will allow you to perform miracles. It will bring you a life of happiness and a life free from illness. You can have everything you want. You will be able to create anything you can visualize. You already have this power! However, you need to discover it, understand it, and learn what to do with it. It is the most valuable resource you will ever use. There is a cost associated with the rewards it will bring you. The cost is small compared to what you will receive. What is the cost you wonder? It's a choice you have to make; the choice of acceptance!

The Universe is filled with an endless source of energy that communicates and interacts with all form; both living and non-living. This energy force connects all mankind to one another and to the rest of the physical world. It also connects us through our intentions and thoughts. Since energy is everything (including our thoughts), we create the world we live in through the intention of what we think. When human thought interacts with energy, it can alter form. It can do everything! It can create anything! It can even heal!

All energy interacts with everything that exists. Positive or good energy restores and heals. Negative or bad energy causes damage and illness. The levels of energy we carry can be measured by the light and frequency we emit. The right combination of thought and energy can spontaneously heal any illness in living form. It can also spontaneously materialize any non-living form. Even science is starting to embrace these concepts through Einstein's theory of relating energy to mass, and through the study of quantum physics.

Imagine the space around you buzzing with energy containing particles, information and knowledge. It can do anything. It can be anything. However, it needs to be told what to do; what to be. Now picture yourself as being the master of that energy. You hold the power to tell it what to do; what to become. It is the power of your thought that comes from deep within your divine self. Think of an orchestra comprised of many individuals and their instruments. They are ready to play, but they don't know what to play, and they don't know how to interact with each other. It is only when the conductor arrives to direct them that beautiful music materializes.

Once you fully understand the impact of the things you do, you will know how important you really are to mankind and to the Universe. The results of your actions are what create the life you live. You determine your life by what you think, what you speak, and what actions you take. It is completely in your control through the choices you make.

The Source within you allows you to be an observer. As an observer, you have the power to see anything you want. You can see what you expect rather than what exists. Your intentions and thoughts as an observer affect the energy around you. You change the nature of the energy through your focus on it. The act of observing has the ability to bring form to the seemingly empty space around you.

I invite you to walk with me on this path so that you, mankind, and the Universe can be everything it was intended to be, everything you could imagine it to be. You are here to make sure that happens. All you need to do is your part. Discover this power within yourself and forever walk the path to freedom. Your life will never be the same!

I am writing this book because of my passion and desire for mankind to experience and have everything they deserve. We are here to learn, to experience, and to create. However, we have lost sight of who we are. Never forget that you are Source!

# About the author

Glenn Wolkoff has been a student of life his entire life. He was born and raised in Los Angeles, and educated at California State University Northridge and University of LaVerne Law School. From a very young age, his innate knowledge and wisdom created a sense of fear in others, so that there was a forced separation between him and his family and peers. As a result, he found childhood and early adulthood to be a lonely place. His mother loved him desperately, but couldn't understand why he was so different. A poem she penned about him when he was quite young cites:

*My Glenn, my son; who cares what people think; who cares what it's all about. I only know I love you; to the world I want to shout. How empty our lives would be if you were not around. Your walk is like music, I listen for the sound. Light up my life with your beautiful smile. Your twinkling eyes – this makes life worthwhile. I'll always be proud to say I gave birth to Glenn that hot summer day.*

That vast space and the quietude of loneliness enabled Wolkoff to hone his skills in observation. He found observing the interaction of people with each other, their environment and planet to be particularly interesting.

Wolkoff's professional work in healthcare facilitated another opportunity to study the many incarnations of the human condition and impart some of the lessons and messages that are part of The Power to coworkers and clients.

He noted people were like magnets: Some were attracted to the directness and truth of his compelling message, and he would find his office frequently filled with people who just wanted to be around him. Others, especially those who don't seek facts or truth and prefer to have drama punctuate their everyday existence, were repelled by him, rejecting him and his process. The most interesting observation seems now to occur frequently – when one of those who have rejected him, suddenly reverse polarity and acknowledge: "You were right."

Wolkoff's profound wisdom is communicated in simple terms that make it easily comprehended and applied to people at all levels of understanding. As a result, his teaching has already helped countless people find greater awareness, opportunity and fulfillment in their day to day life. The awakened awareness has enabled many of his audience to find personal happiness by applying The Power to their daily lives, improving both their physical existence and the health and bounty of their planet.

# Author's note for clarification:

I choose to use the word "Universe" rather than "World" or "Earth." The Universe is all matter and energy, including the World and Earth. It represents all created things; the realm in which all things exist and take place. It is the whole body of things, including the world of human experience.

# Table of Contents

# Chapter 1:    The Power

"What lies before us and what lies behind us are small compared to what lies within us. And when we bring what is within us out into the world, miracles happen."

Henry David Thoreau

Throughout history wars have been fought and lives have been lost over the pursuit of power. It must be important to people if they are willing to destroy each other in order to have it. What is it?

According to the dictionary, the word *"pow-er"* is a noun and means:

1. The ability or capacity to perform or act effectively;
2. Strength or force exerted or capable of being exerted;
3. The ability or official capacity to exercise control;
4. Authority;
5. Having great influence or control over others.

The word power derives from the French word *"poeir"* which means to be able to act. The ability or capacity to act effectively, INCLUDING knowing when <u>not to act</u> is most effective.

Imagine that!

Nations have been willing to destroy each other over something that can be obtained by simply not doing anything; by not acting.

Mankind has misinterpreted the meaning of power and how to obtain it. People will tell you that having lots of money is power; having a title in the workplace is power; being strong is power; or even waiving a gun at people gives one power.

You don't often hear people talk about power being things like knowledge, calmness, quiet, or how one's word is a display of power.

For purposes of this book, none of the above definitions is the kind of power I am talking about.

The power I want you to understand is something that you already have. It is inherent to your being. It was given to you by Source and it lives within you. It is the greatest power anyone can ever imagine. You can do everything with it. You can have anything with it. It is the greatest gift of mankind. What is this power I am talking about?

FREE WILL

Free will is the ability or discretion to choose!
Power is the freedom to act; or, make those choices!

The world we live in is the world we choose.
We live the way we choose to live.
We see what we choose to see.
It is our choices that define our world.
Life is a process of choices!

In *Man's Search For Meaning*, Viktor Frankl wrote:

"We who lived in concentration camps can remember the men who walked through the hut comforting others, giving away their last piece of bread. They may have been few in number, but they offered sufficient proof that everything can be taken from a man but one thing; the last of human freedoms --- to choose one's attitude in any given set of circumstances, to choose one's own way…And there were always choices to make. Every day, every hour, offered the opportunity to make a decision, a decision which determined whether you would or would not submit to those powers which threatened to rob you of your very self, your inner freedoms; which determined whether or not you will become the plaything of circumstance, renouncing freedom and dignity to become molded into the form of the typical inmate."

The few men that Frankl described, the prisoners that were able to exercise their free will under the most heinous of conditions were powerful. They were able to retain and in fact strengthen their power, no doubt, to the dismay of their captors. Although all of the prisoners possessed the same power, only a few of them chose to exercise it.

Like those prisoners, each and every one of you possesses the greatest power in the Universe. The power of free will. The power to choose. The power to make free choices that are unconstrained by internal and external circumstances.

Free will is the ability to select a course of action; the power of acting or of not acting, according to the determination of your will. It is unlimited. You can choose to be happy in life, or not. You can choose to be healthy in life, or not. These are all choices you are free to make. It's really quite simple: If you don't like your life situation, choose differently.

There is only one guideline you must follow when exercising this gift you have been blessed with; and that is, to own the moral responsibility for any action. You must have the willingness to do the right thing.

I suggest to you that you follow my "HILTH" philosophy when choosing to act.

**H**onor
**I**ntegrity
**L**oyalty
**T**rust
**H**onesty

We all know what these words mean and if every choice we made in life followed the meaning of these words, the Universe would not be in the current situation it is in. The root issue is self-discipline and control.

Your Source has given you this gift with the expectation that you would follow the natural law of right behavior; right action gets right results. Right action would be a "HILTH" response to whatever happens. Although this power allows you to behave as you choose, it does not grant you the right to behave in an irrational or irresponsible manner.

The Universe we live in is filled with choices people have made based on non-truth, emotion, distortions of logic, greed, ego, and personal motive. In other words, actions not based on "HILTH."

We are all suffering because of these actions. The lessons learned throughout history are that any gift we have been given, any power we possess, can be used for both good things and for not-good things. Again, it is your choice.

Freedom is not the right to behave as you choose, but rather, the right to make good choices. Choices based on the common good. Choices based on fact. Choices based on reality. Choices not based on emotion or habit and not based on personal motives. Choices not based on illogical thought or distortions of reality.

It all comes back to making good and correct choices. Correct choices are those based on rational and honest thought, or choices based on "HILTH."

So, why are things the way they are today? It all comes back to the root cause I mentioned earlier. The issue of self-discipline and control. Let's explore this a little more.

In 1976, B. F. Skinner wrote:

"It is now widely recognized that great changes must be made in the American way of life. Not only can we not face the rest of the world while consuming and polluting as we do, we cannot for long face ourselves while acknowledging the violence and chaos in which we live. The choice is clear; either we do nothing and allow a miserable and probably catastrophic future to overtake us, or we use our knowledge about human behavior to create a social environment in which we shall live productive and creative lives and do so without jeopardizing the chances that those who follow us will be able to do the same."

The quote is taken from the preface to Skinner's _Walden Two_, a fictional depiction of a society in which human problems are solved through appropriate human conduct. Unfortunately, when you look around today and see what's happening, these words start to sound more like a non-fictional accounting.

Back to the issue of self-discipline and control.

To be able to do the right thing and to make the right decisions, you must gain mastery over yourself. Mastering others is a display of strength; mastering yourself is true power, and eminently powerful.

You control your thoughts and emotions through the realization that you are able to choose what you think and choose how you feel. Many of the thoughts and emotions you have are not your own, but ones that have been imposed upon you from your external environment. To truly be in control means to not be swayed by the conditions you find yourself in, because your state of being is never circumstance-dependent. It is a state of being; a state of consciousness.

Everything in the Universe is energy. Words, thoughts, feelings are also energy. Actions are expressions of energy. The problem most people have is that they focus their energy more on what they do not have rather than on what they have. If you are struggling financially, you will never generate money by concentrating on the fact that you do have any. Focus on the lack, and the lack of money will increase. It's a simple theory.

Through recognizing what you have, you begin to focus your energy on the having of something, instead of the lack of something. If you find yourself needing something, examine why it is that you need it. Be honest about your feelings. If you want something, but your feelings are focused on the lack of it, you will repel the very thing that you hope to draw to yourself.

Look at your life and focus on the qualities that are currently present in your life. Through focusing on what you already have, you allow those qualities to grow and expand. Concentrating on what you have and finding the happiness that is already present will result in the rest of your wants to come your way.

Remember that what you think will eventually become the words you speak. What you speak will eventually become how you act. And, how you act will ultimately determine your destiny and the life you live.

This is a good time to review what we know at this point.

1. Power is the ability to choose your own actions.
2. Remember moral responsibility when you make those choices by practicing "HILTH."

3. Right actions achieve right results.

4. Control your thoughts and emotions so actions chosen are pure and untainted.

5. Remember self-discipline and control when situations present themselves on your doorstep.

6. How you react to any situation is ALWAYS your choice.

7. Focus on what you have rather than on what you lack.

You were created by Source with the expectation that you will follow the natural law of right behavior. Do not let anything stray you from this path. You are here in this life because you choose to be. You need to live your life to the best of your ability and live each moment as fully as possible. You always have free will and the power to choose.

There is a law of natural attraction in the Universe that brings things to you based on the energies you project out. When you focus on what you lack you will discover that other people who are not happy because they focus on what they lack are attracted to you. Lack becomes what defines your inner circle of acquaintances and lack begins to fill your thoughts. This is not where you want to be. Everyone knows that misery loves company.

Positive thoughts and behaviors will attract others with positive thoughts and behaviors. This is where you want to be. The Universe brings back to you that which you have sent out. It is known by some as the law of Karma, but more commonly known as "what you sow is what you shall reap." Who you associate with is also your choice. Make sure you choose people that create a positive environment and enhance your current state of being.

You create your life and your destiny through the choices you make. If you are not happy, choose to be happy and then follow a path of actions to fulfill that desire. What you project is what comes your way.

These are troubled times we live in today. They are caused by people making bad choices based on impure and tainted thoughts; people putting personal agendas ahead of the common good; or people not following "HILTH." These actions have negative consequences for all of us. Consequences will be discussed later in Chapter 6.

Now is the time for change, and that change begins with every one of us making the right choices and taking the right actions. Also note that actions without commitment are not enough. They are false! Here's an example:

Before I married my wife, I knew many things about her, and I knew I loved her very much. We spoke often and we got together as often as we could. We spent holidays together, gave each other gifts, and were very much considered a "couple." We continued to do those things even after I asked her to marry me, but none of those things made us married. I wasn't married until I made my covenant with her on our wedding day, when I took a leap of faith and said "I do." Then, in that moment, I was married. That day, I changed from believing about her, to believing in her, and believing in us. And from that day forward, my actions regarding her are true, based on the commitment of our marriage.

Mankind is at a fork in the path of the Universe. Which way will it choose to go? You have the power to change it all. Anything you can imagine is possible for you to experience and have, through the choices you make. It all starts with you.

Choose wisely!

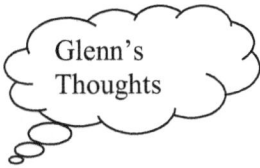

I am an observer by nature. I pay close attention to people's behavior both in the work environment and in the personal environment. The greatest power we have been blessed with is the power to make decisions; the free will to choose. As I watch people in their day-to-day activities, I notice that they struggle with the gift of making decisions. This concerns me.

When I observe people in decision-making situations, they seem confused, sometimes frustrated, afraid to act, and most often they just don't know what to do. This all puzzles me. From the time you are a little child, you decide what to do through observation and knowledge. If you decided incorrectly there were consequences, and you learned from the experience. If you decided correctly there were consequences, and you also learned from the experience. It is a very natural process. So, why do people have such a hard time making decisions?

I think people suffer from "clutter" of the mind. Decision-making is neither simple nor a natural process when the mind is cluttered. Clutter is stuff that needs to be cleared out of your mind. It interferes with the thinking process. It is not anything you need. When you open your closet and everything falls out on you, you rid the closet of its clutter. Most of it ends up being thrown away. Likewise, when you can't think clearly enough to make a decision; you need to rid your mind of its clutter. Most of it ends up being erased from your memory.

I propose this to you. Each time you have to make a decision, you need to ask yourself three simple questions:

1. Why am I doing this?
2. Is it the right thing to do?
3. Is it based on truth?

If you can't satisfactorily answer these three questions, then your decision needs to be to <u>not act</u> until you have the answers to the questions. Any other thoughts in your mind are not relevant to your decision, and are therefore clutter. Decisions based on drama, emotion, fear, or expectations of others, are decisions based on clutter. Clutter should never be a basis for your decision-making process.

It's okay to not act when you can't answer the three questions. It's also okay to not speak when you can't answer the same questions: Why am I saying this? Is it the right thing to say? And, Am I speaking based on truth? Whenever I have forgotten to follow these guidelines, I regret that I have spoken. I have never regretted being silent. Never forget that restraint is also a great power. Don't ever let someone or something make you angry. When you allow that to happen, you have allowed yourself to be conquered. It takes away your power of choice because your actions and words become based on the anger.

Since your life is determined by your decisions and actions, you need to quickly find the answers to the three questions so you can act or speak and move on. Your decisions result in the changes you want to see in your life. They also result in the changes you want to see in the Universe. Delay your decisions only long enough to find the answers you need.

I often wonder, whatever happened to the concept of **wisdom**; the ability to judge correctly and follow the best course of action based on knowledge and understanding. Wisdom is understanding the consequences of your actions and words BEFORE you act or speak. You have the ability to process information, just make sure that the information you use, is always based on truth. Then, simply decide to do the right thing with the truth you have. I want everyone to be able to think clearly, and be free from clutter. Be wise!

I also wish that all people would place a high priority on **honor** which is about placing a premium on the qualities of good behavior. Honor is about commitment to the underlying values in your thoughts and actions. It's more than just doing the right thing; it's being known and trusted in the community for always doing the right thing. How many people do you know that are willing to put the welfare of the community above their loyalty to specific individuals? It's a hard choice to make.

I can only dream that some day all mankind will have thoughts that are pure, clear, and based on truth. All behavior will then be right and we will be moving in the direction of making life in the Universe as it was intended to be.

# Chapter 2:    Truth

"And ye shall know the truth,
and the truth shall make you free."

John 8:32

According to the dictionary, the word *"truth"* is a noun and means:

1. the actual state of being;
2. being in accord with fact and reality;
3. truth is that which is.

The legal definition of truth is:

1. the actual state of things;
2. *res ipsa loquitur* – the thing speaks for itself.

And then there is the philosophical definition:

1. truth simply exists;
2. what is just is.

As you can see, this is going to be a bit more difficult than power. In the Universe, the concept of truth has become so convoluted that many claim it no longer exists. It has been said that based on the current state of things, the truth can no longer be identified. With that said, I strongly disagree.

I propose to you that the truth is knowable. It can be perceived by the physical senses and understood by the mind. Those who do the right thing shall know the truth. And yes, the truth shall make you free.

You were created by Source. You come from Source. Source is a part of you. You are a part of Source. It has long been accepted that Source is the truth. Since you are Source, recognize that you are the truth.

Accept that you are the truth!

Some time ago there was a very wise man that walked our Universe preaching to believe in the truth he spoke. You all know who he is. When asked directly; "What is truth?" he responded with a stare and silence. He was for sure a very wise man. However, as recorded in John 14:17, he spoke of the spirit of truth as being within us.

"Even the spirit of truth; whom the world cannot receive, because it seeth him not, neither knoweth him: but ye know him; for he dwelleth with you, and shall be in you."

In more modern words; the spirit of truth. The world cannot accept him, because it neither sees him nor knows him. But you know him, for he lives with you and in you.

Again, Source is truth. You are Source. You are the truth.

So, what does this all mean?

You have the freedom and the power to choose to know the truth. To choose to know yourself and discover who and what you are. No one can do that for you. Only you can do it.

The subject of truth is essential to understanding mankind. Although the existence of truth is deceptive, it is clear that the absence of truth, or non-truth, is falsehood. In the Universe many key decisions are being made on non-truths. Wars are being fought based on falsehoods. Businesses are taking your money based on falsehood. Medical cures and treatments are being offered based on falsehoods.

How and why is this happening? It goes back to decisions being made without moral responsibility. Is the Universe intentionally deceiving us? Sometimes yes, but more often no. Not telling the truth does not always mean you are telling a lie. Often people believe that what they are doing and saying is the truth even though it is not. And, unfortunately, sometimes people are fully aware that it is a falsehood. When you intentionally deceive, you are lying. When you believe what you say is the truth, and it is not, you are not lying. In either case the end result is the same.

People who believe what they say to be the truth when it is not are who concern me more than people who lie. Mankind has become very good at fooling itself into believing what is true. It's because we see what we want to see, know only what we choose to know, and believe what is convenient. It is a character of laziness and taking the path of least resistance.

Often today, people are making life decisions and business decisions based on emotion rather than on fact. You need to spend time and effort questioning things and investigating things in order to get to the truth. It requires work. But, it must be done.

Moses Maimonides was a preeminent medieval scholar on truth. Maimonides said, "The truth does not become more true by virtue of the fact that the entire world agrees with it, nor less so, even if the whole world disagrees with it."

Truth exists, regardless of who knows or does not know about it. If a million people believe something to be true, it will not be truth, unless it already is without any believers. What is true is independent of who knows. It does not become a non-truth merely because someone misrepresents it. This is why it is so important to look inside yourself to find truth.

Truth always exists in a pure state. It is discovered through knowledge, through investigation, through asking right questions, and through a journey of self-discovery. Since you typically believe what you tell yourself, you need to immediately stop self-deception. Even though you may not want to deal with truth, because it is easier not to, self-deception will hold you back from living an abundant life.

Other people, circumstances, events, and material things are not what make you happy. What you believe about these things is what determines your happiness or unhappiness. Behaving and acting on what you believe, without verification of truth, creates bad decisions and mistakes in your life. You need to act on truth! As you discover the truth, negative thoughts will be replaced by positive thoughts.

Truth is an experience of the extreme depths of the self. It is total identification with what is. Truth is what it is. Here's an example to illustrate my point:

You are on a cross-country journey when the small aircraft you are on suffers an engine failure. The captain has already announced that if you stay on the airplane, you will not survive. He offers you one chance to save yourself when he shows you a parachute. You have seen people skydive successfully wearing parachutes, so you believe about parachutes and how they work, but, jumping out of that crashing aircraft with one on your back requires more than a mental belief. It requires an active response of your will. To be saved by the parachute, you must first believe in it so that you strap it on your back, jump out of the aircraft and pull the ripcord. When you jump out, it will carry you to safety. If you jump out of the aircraft with just the faith in a parachute, but no parachute, it's not enough and your landing is really going to hurt. To take it one step further, you must have the right parachute strapped on your back. <u>A faulty substitute cannot save you.</u>

Mankind is lost in a Universe plagued with falsehoods and drama. Why is this? We have chosen to not investigate things and to not seek the truth. We do not question things; and instead, we seek immediate gratification and rewards. Investigation begins with your own inner being. Unless you know yourself, all of your knowledge lacks authenticity.

Past civilizations were destroyed by external attack. Our civilization is destroying itself by the internal threat of inappropriate behavior. In other words, actions chosen not based on truth. We are destroying ourselves by not following the natural laws of behavior. I cannot stress the importance of starting to look inside yourself to find the truth so that you can make rational choices in life. If it is not right, do not do it. If it is not true, do not speak it. It's that simple!

Every action you take is reflected in the Universe in a greatly magnified form. It changes the Universe! The root of all social degeneration is with each individual mind that exists. Before we change the world, we need to change ourselves and how we think.

When you are out of tune with yourself, your mind lives in chaos and knows no harmony. You can only take harmony back by looking inside and calming the mind with truth. Once you become in harmony with yourself, your outer actions will reflect that accord with the Universe. It is a natural process. Whatever is within us is what flows from us; it is what we give out. It will also be what we receive.

Mankind is blinded by ambition. Everyone wants to be something other than who they are. We have forgotten who we really are. To be something more than who we are is not possible. The pursuit of power without truth is a root cause of illness in a society.

Freedom and independence are not obtained through falsehoods in life. You must be willing to face the truth within yourself and right your own wrongs. Freedom and independence lie in the knowledge of truth. And it is truth, and truth alone, that makes you free.

Truth will always guide you in the appropriate direction. Truth liberates!

So, why do people lie? The main reason is fear of vulnerability, which includes fear of being held accountable, fear of disappointing, fear of being caught, fear of losing something and the list goes on and on. People think it is okay to tell people what they want to hear. And, many people intentionally deceive for personal motive and greed.

Mark Twain said, "Always tell the truth. That way, you don't have to remember what you said." The burden one places on themselves when they lie is extremely self-destructive. You become trapped in your world of lies and have to continue supporting them with more lies. It soon becomes your reality that you live in and eventually everyone will know. So do yourself a favor and stop and come clean. Your life will appreciate it. The Universe will appreciate it.

As stated earlier, people who lie are not the ones that concern me the most; those who speak falsehoods and believe them to be true are more troublesome to me. We all allow this behavior by not questioning things, and not digging for answers. It really is a sign of laziness, and is directly attributed to life today being "drama" driven. People jump to conclusions, people misinterpret, people get excited easily, and people react on emotion rather than on fact.

Mark Twain also said, "A lie can travel halfway around the world, while the truth is putting on its shoes."

Both business life and personal life is plagued with emotionally based decisions. I saw it all the time in business meetings. People meet to solve a problem and as a result assignments are handed out, business processes are changed, and peoples' jobs are affected. I sit and listen and then ask some specific questions about the problem only to find no one has any answers. No one had researched the problem to determine what really happened, no one had facts, and no one knew the truth. More often than not, once things were investigated, you discover that the problem wasn't what you thought it was. In other words, the real problem was something other than what you were discussing. These same scenarios take place in personal relationships all the time. I again stress the importance to you of how critical it is to seek the truth before you act.

So many decisions in the Universe have been made on non-truth; and, more decisions have been made on top of those decisions, that it becomes a task similar to peeling away the layers of an onion to get back to the core truth.

Look around the Universe, listen to peoples' conversations, watch the news, read the headlines on your computer.....how much of it is drama; of little importance to your everyday life? Drama is everywhere. People have come to love drama because it is an excuse to not deal with real life and its issues. This needs to change!

Before we leave the subject of truth, I need to mention one other thing. You need to rid yourself of ego. Ego neither listens nor thinks. It retains information and continues to believe the falsehoods it has already accepted. Ego is the false self. You cannot know the truth when you have ego.

You must experience the knowledge you have to determine its truth. Remember; right behavior, right actions, and choices based on truth!

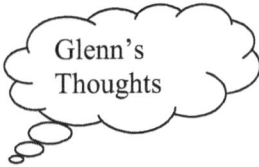

Glenn's
Thoughts

I think most people find it easier to live by benign tolerance than to become involved in the messy process of seeking truth and holding people accountable for their actions. I have devoted my life to pursuing the truth behind the thoughts I believe in. I know that the key to mankind's happiness is to know the truth.

If I had to pick a subject from my book that I am most passionate about, it would be "truth." I have witnessed so many people ruin the life they live because of their refusal to acknowledge truth. People love to tell stories. They think it makes them more interesting, more important, more likable, or even more lovable. Unfortunately, over time, these stories become people's realities. Once that happens, they become lost in the falsehoods they created and believe in. They base key life decisions on those falsehoods and they enter and terminate relationships based on those falsehoods. Life becomes a grand delusion with only one way out; to accept and embrace the truth.

Stop defining who and what you are through the eyes of others. You, and only you, need to understand who you are and live the life you are intended to live. Follow your own path and most of all, love yourself. However, you can't accomplish any of this if you do not use truth as the basis of your every thought, every spoken word, and every action taken. When you base your choices or actions on falsehood, you will always do the wrong thing. You will never be happy if you live your life in the stories you create rather than the reality you need to accept. This is why and how the truth sets you free.

The Universe is full of people who tell lies. Remember that a lie is intentionally misrepresenting the truth. People accept those lies as truth and act on them. Those actions always lead to unfavorable results because they are not based on truth. People have many reasons for the lies they tell. Whatever reason they come up with is irrelevant; this behavior only complicates their life in a negative way.

They think they fool others into believing what they say is the truth; however, the only person they fool is themselves. Falsehoods always find a way of being discovered. Trust me, it will happen. And, you will have made your life, and the lives of others around you, one of suffering.

As mentioned in this chapter, the people who tell lies are not the ones that concern me most. They are ill and everyone around them will know it sooner or later. The real danger to society is caused by people who believe they speak the truth but do not. You are partly responsible for this danger perpetuating because you allow it. You need to learn to question information, investigate information, and take the time to find the facts behind what people say. It's a simple process but it requires some responsibility and effort on your part. Once again, trust me. It's worth it.

A large portion of the economic financial crisis we are all experiencing is attributed to people telling lies in order to take your money for their own personal greed. As much as they are to blame, the victims of the fraud allowed it to happen. They believed the stories they were told because they wanted to believe their money would multiply quickly. People didn't question what they were told because they didn't want it to be false. If people who are offered these "too good to be true" deals asked the right questions to find the truth, they would have discovered the truth and not invested their money. You have an obligation to protect yourself through discovery of the truth. If everyone did this, the people who lie to defraud you of your money would quickly be out of business. They are successful only because they get you to make decisions and take actions based on falsehoods, rather than on truth.

The good thing about asking the right questions and investigating facts is that it works for people who tell lies, and for people who unknowingly misrepresent the truth. Any decision and action you make in life that is not based on truth is one that you will wish you had not made. The consequences will always be negative. You need to also understand that once you go down the path of seeking truth, you may learn things that you would rather not know. No matter how awful or discerning the truth is, you are always better off because you know it. Whatever decision you have to make because of what you discover will at least be a decision based on truth. I will be the first to tell you that learning the truth is often a painful process. However, it will always eventually be more painful if you don't base your life on truth.

I am often amazed at the things people believe. It is sometimes so obvious and ridiculous that I wonder how they can not see the truth. It's because they do not want to see the truth. If ever you base your actions on what you believed to be truth and later discover your belief was wrong, simply make a new decision based on truth and move on with your life. If you choose to ignore the truth because it is a more difficult path to take, then you have again made a decision based on falsehood. You have now compounded your original error. You need to become humble to learn and accept truth. Remember that part of your freedom to choose is what allows you to pursue truth. It's a choice you make.

As I was working on this section of the book, the news was buzzing with talk of a "swine flu" pandemic. As I listened to what government officials and news reporters were saying, I realized that this was a demonstration of how common it is for people to speak falsehoods without knowing it. And, these people were professionals; people that society relies on for valid information. Their comments were filled with drama, emotion, fear, and incorrect information. Not a single person had taken the time to find the truth before speaking. Was it really a pandemic? Did it come from pigs? Do you catch it from eating pork? Is it safe to travel? Should we keep our children away from the zoo? If this is a pandemic, will millions of people die?

People were creating their own answers to these questions because of all the confusion being communicated. Questions without answers because spoken words not based on truth were being spread. You would have thought that these professionals would have spent a lot of time behind closed doors getting the truth before ever speaking a word to the public. Unfortunately, being the first to report was more important. After about a week of this, it was announced that the flu virus that was frightening the world is beginning to look a lot less threatening.

It wasn't the flu virus that frightened the world; it was the people reporting it.

# Chapter 3:    Who are you?

"You are the image of Source."

Glenn Wolkoff

"If men could only know each other,
they would neither idolize nor hate."

Elbert Hubbard

Think about the last time you had a dire health emergency and ended up in the hospital. As soon as you arrived, essentially, your title and importance were stripped away. Instead, you become identified by the line of numbers or bar code on a plastic band that is riveted around your wrist. Your own clothing, uniform, or power suit was removed and replaced by a thin cotton robe that barely covers your back. Additionally, you discover you have lost your individuality; you are dressed exactly as all the other patients wearing wristbands. Layer by layer, you have been stripped of the icons and trappings of your false self. Your history is gone; your salary and title are immaterial; and your rank among your peers is determined by things that are totally outside your control. You are no longer your job, your title, your dramas, your life. To those around you, you are the cardiac arrest in bed number seven. As you lay under the bright examination lights, you begin to realize you are not your job. You are not the car you drive. Your address or zip code has no importance. The school you went to is not a consideration. All of that is gone; it is inconsequential. So, who are you then?

Most people out there are busy promoting themselves, protecting themselves, projecting their false selves --- titles, positions, jockey for power and favor. Everything falls short of representing themselves, because they do not know who they are.

When you ask most people who they are, they answer with their name. "I am Bob." You are not your name. Everything has a label today. So, really, who are you?

YOU are a spiritual being. YOU are Source. YOU are energy. You exist independently and collectively. You are awake, alive, cognizant and conscious. You have a mind that operates outside the physical Universe; however, you are connected to a body which operates only in the physical Universe.

Don't quit on me now; I know the last paragraph was a mindful. Keep what I said in your thoughts as you continue reading.

Let's go back to that great wise man that walked the Universe long ago. The one everyone knows. He spoke of the "trinity." Through his words we interpreted the trinity to be the Father, Son, and Holy Spirit. Further interpretations accepted what he said as representing Source as father, he as the son of Source and spirit. Three distinct entities.

He knew exactly what he was talking about; he preached it and he taught it at every opportunity. We misunderstood it. He was not talking about three distinct entities. He was talking about a set of three that forms a single unit. That unit is YOU.

You were created by Source to be the image of Source. You are Source. And, Source is you. Everything is connected through energy. In fact, all life form in the Universe is connected through energy. It's all one!

You are a spirit and a mind connected to a body. Your spirit is the true ethereal you. Your mind is non-physical. And your physicality is the manifestation of the spirit and mind. Remember that thought and energy creates reality. The wise man came here to teach you that you are a spiritual being with a thinking mind having human experiences through a physical body. You are "thinking energy." He also wanted to demonstrate that Source continues to live with or without a body. I will keep saying that you are Source over and over again. Your spirit is the actual energy that started the whole process of your existence. You are made up of a spirit, a mind, and a body. Your true self is your spirit and your mind which are non-physical; however, you are connected to a body which enables you to experience the physical Universe.

Your body allows you to experience the pleasures of the senses; touch, taste, smell, sight and sound. It also allows you to experience the pain of illness and disease.

So, back to the question of; who are you?

You are a spiritual being with a mind; made of energy; in the image of Source. You are Source. You have the same capabilities as Source. You are eternal. One more thing; all spiritual beings are connected through energy. So where does the body figure into all of this? Your body is the vehicle that connects you to the physical Universe. The body is temporary and is not who you are.

Just as a plant cannot survive without its roots, you cannot survive without your spirit.

Spirit or energy is the source of all creation. The mind or mental process is the beginning of a physical manifestation and the body ultimately becomes the physical manifestation of the thought process. You are a non-physical consciousness that is experiencing physical reality.

Believe it or not; you are here at this time because you choose to be.

There are four laws of creation:
1. You exist;
2. You are Source; Source is You;
3. What you put out is what you get back;
4. Change is the only constant.

You are an eternal being and while you may change your form, you cannot cease to exist.

Let's talk about the mind for a little bit. Its true purpose is to store data, experience, and of course learn so it can evolve. There are five stages to the mind:

1. The **conscious** mind holds all the information you need to accomplish what you are currently doing.
2. The **subconscious** mind allows you to store acquired knowledge and experience for later recall.
3. The **super conscious** mind is where thoughts are turned into actualities.
4. The **unconscious** mind contains experiences you do not wish to remember.
5. The **body mind** monitors all of your body's functions and sensations.

As you can see, the mind is very powerful with all its unique functions operating in good harmony with one another. With an organized focus, visualizations will manifest in the physical Universe. Your spirit allows you to create an intention that creates a concept or idea in the mind that can be unleashed at any time you choose to use it. Anything you can imagine is possible for you to experience. You have the power to create your own Universe as it should be. Remember, you always have free will and freedom to choose.

I'd like to spend some time talking about "essence" (not the kind that you add to your bath water.)

All spiritual beings have essence which is the inner qualities you are born with. Being in your essence is being in your essential nature. It is being fully present in spirit, mind and body. It is being the whole you. Your personality is not who you are; that is external learned behavior and frequently conflicts with essence.

Essence carries with it a variety of sensations. They can be referred to as essence states or core states because they are a part of you. There may be a sensation of love, wholeness, serenity, beingness, unity, acceptance and power. Each of these sensations is already part of your essential self. When you search for these qualities external to your self without first finding them in yourself, your experience will most likely not be successful. These qualities are far more powerful when you encounter them in your essential self. They are always present and available for you to discover.

If you think about it, it stands to reason that if you do not love yourself you cannot love someone else. Also if you are not happy internally, the odds are slim that someone else can make you happy. Finding these essence states inside yourself will provide you with a sense of being deeply nourished. Once these essences become experiences, they can be healing, spiritual, and transformative. You were given everything you need in life inside of yourself; you need very little externally.

Operating from essence equates to being fully present in your body, having a good sense of choice, perceiving the world clearly, having a positive sense about yourself, being connected with your intuitive state, and understanding all of your essence qualities.

Essence is being without the boundaries of time of space. It is your spirit and consciousness; your energetic being independent of your body. By the way, spirits can be young, mature, old, and eventually transcendental and infinite without bodies.

This is why it is so important in life to do the right thing, make the hard choices, take the path less traveled, and most of all act only on truth. To not do these things takes you out of your essence and away from your self into a life filled with bad choices, drama, falsehoods, and unhappiness.

So many people are operating out of essence that all of these wrong choices and wrong actions are jeopardizing the Universe we live in.

People lack self-discipline and control! You cannot let freedom destroy the inner disciplines that make it possible. A powerful morality and sense of values are essential for freedom to work. Otherwise, it becomes a democracy without participation, a freedom without sacrifice, and prosperity without hard work.

There is also the Michael theory of essence that is very interesting. The Michael theory is that there are seven primary essence types that exist. Each of us has chosen one of those essence types as our primary trait of who we are. Determining your essence type and living a life aligned with your essence will assist you to be in harmony with yourself. The seven essence types are:

1.  Server: Service-oriented, dedicated, loving, helps those who are suffering. Servers tend to be nurses, veterinarians, office workers, housekeepers, organizers, etc.

2.  Priest: Inspired, visionary, and zealous leaders and troubleshooters. Priests tend to be teachers, non-profit foundation leaders, and workers in industries that are compassionate.

3.  Artisan: Highly creative, musical, artistic, dreamers. Artisans tend to be carpenters, communicators, artists, fashion models, designers, musicians and poets.

4. <u>Sage</u>: Humorous, flamboyant, center of attention, masters of expressionism. Sages tend to be actors, sales people, politicians, comedians, creative journalists (as opposed to hard news journalists).

5. <u>Warrior</u>: Solid, brave, strong, valorous, protectors. Warriors tend to be lawyers, career military personnel, prison guards, athletes, police officers.

6. <u>King</u>: Natural leader, regal, promoters of ceremony. Typical Kings are CEOs, successful entrepreneurs, head coaches, holders of high political offices.

7. <u>Scholar</u>: Neutral, research-oriented, collector, sorter and communicator of information, student of life. Typical scholars are doctors, astrologers, scientists, academicians, writers, legal counselors.

There are many resources available to help you determine which of the seven your primary essence is. You may already know.

Let's stop and take a quick review of what we know so far about who you are.

You were created by Source in Source's own image; You are Source. You are a spirit and a mind connected to a physical body. You have a duty to act like Source. You have an obligation to do the right thing based on truth. Essentially you are a spiritual being having human experiences in a physical world. If you understand who you are and follow your chosen path, everything will be as it was intended to be. Each of you has your own path to Source.

The new Universe lies inside of each of you; however, if you choose to not know yourself, then you will dwell in poverty. Wake Up! It's time to discover who you are and fulfill your destiny and claim your prosperity. The Universe is counting on it.

As Socrates said, "Know thyself."

I hope you understand me when I tell you that you are
Source and that you are truth. Everything in the Universe is
energy. You are a spiritual being comprised of energy. You
have a thinking mind that controls that energy. Therefore,
you are a spirit and a mind that is "thinking energy." That
is who you are. You were created in the image of Source;
therefore, you are Source. Your physical body's sole
purpose is to allow you to experience physical life. It is not
who you are.

Because everything and everyone is energy, we are all
connected to each other. We are all energy; we are all
connected; and we are all Source. Then what makes us
different from one another? We all have our own unique
path to Source. This is why it is so important to know who
you are and find your path in life. It is the only uniqueness
you have as an individual.

Knowing who you are and understanding who you are is a truth only you can know. It is your truth. Once you know yourself, you know truth. This is why, you are truth.

Each of us is here for a reason. The sooner you find your reason and begin your journey toward that goal, the sooner you will find true happiness. Everything else in life that you believe will make you happy is going to turn out to be a falsehood. Your financial wealth, your material belongings, other people, and your career is not going to make you happy. You may think it is, but the only thing that will bring you true happiness is knowing who you are and living that life. Once you have found that happiness, everything else will enhance your enjoyment of that happiness. However, you first must be content with yourself.

For those who do not know who they are, the material things and financial wealth is all that they have. It is their false life. They cling to it and will do anything to keep it. Without it they are nothing. Unfortunately, they will never know happiness. On the other hand, those who know who they are and are living that life, will greatly enjoy their material things and financial wealth, but their lives are the same with or without those things.

Because everyone has a role in society, all people need to be respected for who they are, and no one person should ever be idolized.

Accept that you are eternal and you are not your body. Discover your true self! Enjoy being who you are! Have a hunger for your truth! Make all the right choices! Do all the right things! Be happy! And, most of all, BE YOU!!

# Chapter 4:    You are not your body

"There is more to life than just your body."

Glenn Wolkoff

This chapter is really a continuation of the previous chapter which focused on Who are you? It's important enough to have its own caption, just in case it was not clear to you in the previous chapter.

To put it simply, you are not your body! You are non-physical. Your body is just a vehicle. You will have many bodies in your lifetime.

You are made up of a spirit and a mind. Your spirit is Source and has all the capabilities of Source. You experience things in the physical world through the body you are connected to. You are really "thinking energy."

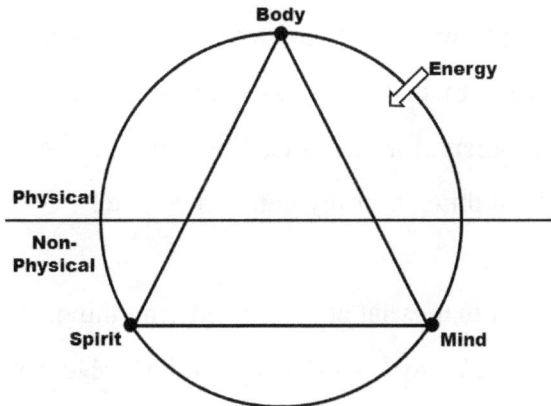

You are immortal; your body is mortal. Think of your body as a dwelling that you live in. Take care of your body because it is where you live. The body really only needs two things to be healthy: nourishment and motion. Proper eating and exercise is really all you need.

Too many people define themselves as their body, just as they define themselves as the car they drive, the house they own, or the job they have. These things are all the same. These things are not you.

We are a society obsessed with our physical existence. We worry about how we look. We worry about aging. Are we pretty, are we not pretty? Are we too heavy, too skinny, too wrinkled? What is the color of our hair? What kind of clothes should we wear? Are we attractive? Are we sexy? We also tend to justify our falsehoods by comparing our body with others, for example, I'm better than he or she is because I am thinner, or my hair is nicer, etc.

Instead of all that, what about considering things like, Am I a good person? Do I do the right things? Do I make the right decisions? Are my actions based on truth? Are you starting to get it!

As stated earlier, your body is a vehicle that links you to the physical world. Your body allows you the pleasures of the physical senses and causes suffering through illness and disease. It is mortal and therefore will die, no matter what you do.

You, on the other hand, are immortal and will exist forever, with or without your body. You are energy. You are Source.

If we spent half the time we direct towards developing our body to developing our spirit and mind; the Universe would be a much better place to live. If I had to prioritize the order of importance and attention we should give ourselves, it would be:

1. Spirit
2. Mind
3. Body

How about that; I put body last on the list. Most people place it first on the list. Some day and I hope some day soon, people are going to understand this. It all starts with acceptance.

You will find that the more you get in touch with your inner self and start to live in your essence, the more things like your body will become less important to you.

As long as you choose to be a part of the physical world, you will have a body to deal with. Keep it pure; keep it clean; keep it healthy. And, please remember to devote a lot of time to your spirit and mind. It needs more attention than your body. After all, your body is a servant of your mind.

It is time for you to embrace your spiritual nature or forever be limited and imprisoned by the constraints of your physical body.

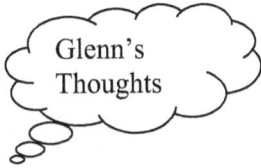

Always remember that you are not your body. You are a spiritual being with a thinking mind. You are energy. You are Source. You will be here forever. Your existence never ends, even though the body you occupy will inevitably die. You will have many bodies throughout your existence.

Please do not define yourself by your body. Your body is not who you are. Your body is merely your connection to the physical world. You exist with it or without it. That, by the way, is your choice.

Your body needs good nourishment, so be wise about what you feed it. And, your body needs moving energy, so be sure to give it a daily dose of motion or exercise. The healthiest exercise for the body is energy motion movement. There are many resources out there that can help you understand what energy motion movement is. Also, everyday life contains necessary movement to keep the body healthy. Do not become physically lazy. Technology has motivated mankind to be lazy. There was once a time when you had to get up to change the channel on your television, or get up to answer the telephone, leave your house to shop, and even walk over to someone's office at work if you needed to talk to them. All this has changed, so people sit a lot more than they should.

I recommend you take walks every day, walk up stairs instead of using the elevator, go places, do yard work, and make everyday life your gymnasium. It's good for you and it's fun. Although you are not your body, you need to keep your body healthy so that it brings you the maximum pleasure and the minimum suffering.

Enjoy the pleasures of the body. See the beauty of the Universe. Hear the music of the universe. Smell the aromas of the Universe. Taste the delicacies of the Universe. And, most of all experience the joys of touch. There is nothing more satisfying in the physical world than holding a hand, a hug, a kiss...enjoy the experience of touching. I stress that you enjoy your physicality, because as much as your body will bring you joy and pleasure, it can also bring you suffering through pain and disease.

It is most important to remember that you are not your body when you are in a physical suffering stage. Always remember that your body takes orders from your mind. It is your body that is in pain, not you! Use the power of your mind to separate yourself from your body when it is in a stage of suffering. Your spirit and mind know no pain unless you fill it with falsehoods. You will discover that when your body is in pain, focusing on being healthy and things you enjoy will help cause the pain to become secondary. Never focus on the pain, and always try to divert your attention through positive energy.

# Chapter 5:    What is your purpose?

"The highest purpose of your life is to evolve into the
person intended by Source."

Glenn Wolkoff

"The greatest waste in the world is the difference between
what we are and what we could become."

Ben Herbster

Remember that Source created you in its own image. Source intended you to be like it and your purpose in life is to evolve into it. In order to accomplish that purpose, you must first know who you are. To become Source you need to be yourself.

We are all connected because we all come from Source and we are all energy. So, the purpose of all mankind's incarnation is to evolve into Source. This is our destiny. And, our life goal is to find our way there.

If you are beginning to see the connection between all of this, then you are on your way to understanding. The next step would be to accept what you now understand.

Let's review!

You were created by Source and your life purpose is to evolve into Source.

You have the freedom to make any choices in life to get there.

Your choices must be based on truth in order to be the right choice.

Life is a process of choices.

You are an energy driven spiritual being that exists forever.

You are connected to the physical world through your body.

You are not your body.

Rumi, a 13th century Persian poet and theologian said, "It is as if a king had sent you to a country to carry out one special, specific task. You go to the country and you perform a hundred other tasks, but if you have not performed the task you were sent for, it is as if you have done nothing at all. So people have come into the world for particular tasks, and that is our purpose. If we don't perform it, we will have nothing."

When all spiritual beings, working in harmony, find their path and fulfill their intent, the optimum mankind, as intended by Source, will exist.

So, if your highest purpose in life is your path to Source, and evolving into the being intended by Source, then you need to be yourself to the best of your ability.

You can start to see why it so important that you know who you are. We talked about your spiritual nature and we talked about your body. Let's talk a bit about your mind.

Before we begin, I need you to be able to accept the following statement. The activities of your mind have no limits. Can you do that?

Presuming you accepted, it is only logical to know that the mind creates the surroundings of your life. A pure mind surrounds itself with pure things and an impure mind surrounds itself with impure things. Things in your life are no more or less limited than your mind. Pure equates to truth while impure equates to falsehood.

If your mind has the right understanding of things, your surroundings become the real state of things. Things you can trust. Things that are truthful. However, if the mind is full of ignorance, falsehood and greed, the world of delusion becomes your environment surrounding you with things that you cannot trust, things that are non-truth.

Whenever things in the Universe appear to be delusional, it is a sign that you need to perform an analysis on your mind. It's sort of a reality check to be sure that you are free from impure thoughts, and that you are not creating your delusional surroundings. No matter what the outcome of your self-analysis; the very process of checking will bring clarity to your mind.

Once you understand that all things are created by your mind, you realize the necessity of having a pure mind. A mind with no predispositions based on non-truth. When you act and speak with a pure mind, the right things will follow you. Your path will be smooth and your journey peaceful.

To achieve your purpose, you must cultivate your mind the same as you would a garden. You can plant all the seeds you want in your garden, but unless you water it, fertilize it, and rid it of weeds, it will not grow. Likewise, you need to feed your mind with knowledge, and rid it of non-truth. This will determine how little or how much abundance you will have in life.

You also need to understand that in life, things are constantly changing. Something that once served a useful purpose may no longer be needed. Thoughts work the same way. Once you use them and they are no longer needed, rid yourself of them. Do not cling to things that you no longer need. Once something is no longer needed, it becomes a burden to keep. Learn to let go of burdensome material things as well as burdensome thoughts.

Here is a story to help illustrate this point.

Long ago, there was a man on a long journey. His travels took him to a path along a river. After tediously hiking, he noticed that the side of the river he was on was very difficult and dangerous terrain; however, the other side seemed much easier and safer. He sat on a rock to consider how he might get across to the other side. He saw a fallen tree just ahead, and from it, he bound branches together with reeds and built a raft that floated him safely across the river. Once there, he saw that the path was indeed much smoother and easier to walk. He looked at his raft, and thought to himself that since it had been very useful for crossing the river, it shouldn't be abandoned. So, despite the fact that it was wet and heavy, he decided to carry it along with him on his back for the rest of his journey.

As you can see, keeping and carrying the raft became an unnecessary burden and he was not being wise to think he still needed it. It had served its purpose.

Like the raft, thoughts that are no longer necessary only serve to clutter your mind. Peace of mind is essential for achieving your purpose. You need to avoid becoming attached to self-indulgence in the physical Universe in order to keep your mind free and able to serve you well.

A pure mind will help you to know yourself and discover who you are. And, knowing who you are will allow you to follow your path of purpose in life.

If you walked into a room with your eyes closed and then opened them, the first thing you will see is the interior of the room. Only later will you see the view outside the windows of the room. People make the mistake of seeing and knowing things external to themselves, before they see who they are. It is not a natural order of things.

Don't fall into the delusion of grasping at external things for your own convenience and comfort. Chasing wealth, treasure, and material things bring you closer and closer to the physical world and further from Source and your purpose in life.

There are those in life who chase everything out there in the material world because they want it all. They define themselves by what they own. These people easily give in to bad thoughts and retain those thoughts forever in their minds. They are connected primarily to the physical

Universe. Then there are those that chase material things but quickly rid themselves of those thoughts and needs. They are connected primarily to the mind Universe. Lastly, there are those whose thoughts come and go with every moment, and are not retained because they have little need for external things. Their minds are always kept pure, open, and undisturbed. They are connected primarily to the spirit Universe.

There is only one way to achieve your purpose. It is done through appropriate behavior. Do the right thing. Make the right decisions. Base all your actions on truth. Know who you are and stay on your path to Source.

You must keep your words, actions, and mind pure. Impure thought leads to impure actions that result in suffering because you move further away from who you are and further away from Source. It is only when you maintain a pure and peaceful mind and continue to act with goodness that you are able to achieve your purpose.

No matter what situation you find yourself in, the way out is to always stay true to yourself. Never let the situation control who you are. Who you are never changes no matter what circumstance comes your way.

Glenn's
Thoughts

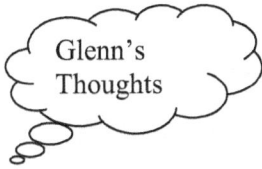

We all have the same universal purpose in life which is to evolve into Source. Since you are already Source, evolving into Source means that you master all the capabilities of Source. Learning how to be free from illness, and how to heal yourself and others, is part of the evolution to becoming Source. Understanding that you are eternal is also part of the journey to Source. Your evolution to becoming Source is one of understanding the truth and accepting who and what you are.

Although each person has the same purpose, their path for getting there is unique. We are all trying to become the image of Source, but we all take a different path to get there. Understanding who you are is what determines the path you take to get there. When you live your life on the right path you will be happy. If you were meant to be a teacher in life and you are a mechanic, you will not be happy. The main cause of unhappiness in people is that they are doing something in life different than the path intended for them. It is you who chose your path when you chose your physical existence. However, as you evolve in your physicality, you soon forget the path you chose. This happens because you become out of harmony and out of balance with your true self.

When all people are on the right path and are being who they were intended to be, the Universe will be in balance and harmony. This is why it is so important to discover who you are. You need to rely on your instincts and intuitive nature. Those are your deepest thoughts. They will help you discover who you are. Once you find your role in life and step into it, you will feel more at peace with yourself. You and everyone else around you will notice the change. Things you once considered important in your life will suddenly become irrelevant.

I ask nothing more from life than to pursue my freedom to share the knowledge that I have come to know and understand. If my book can help make this happen, then I am on my journey to fulfill my path and purpose. I am also counting on YOU to do your part!

# Chapter 6: Consequences

"There are two freedoms --- the false, where a man is free to do what he likes; the true, where he is free to do what he ought."

Charles Kingsley

"There are no rewards or punishments --- only consequences."

William R. Inge

A stone wall does not intentionally hurt you when you punch it. You hurt yourself by not understanding the consequences of striking the wall. The intent of this chapter is to help you understand how important you are in the Universe. Everything you do has an effect on the Universe. Everything you do has consequences.

By the end of this chapter, you will understand why doing the right thing is not just a necessity to achieve your purpose in life, but also a necessity for the survival of mankind and the Universe. You are that important!

Because we are all connected by energy, every time we act, there is a consequence to all mankind. People react to what you do and others react to those reactions. This goes on and on for an infinite number of impacts and actions. The choices you make and actions you take have far-reaching consequences.

This process is known as the "ripple effect." In more simple terms; for every action in the Universe, there is a reaction.

It is exactly the same effect you see when you toss a pebble in the water. The act is tossing the pebble. The action is the impact of the pebble entering the water. The ripple effect are the rings (or ripples) generated from the pebble entering the water. Not just one, two, or three rings; but a series of rings extending out to the limits of the body of water. Keep this concept in your mind as we explore this further.

The smallest action can have consequences that you cannot begin to imagine!

A simple exercise helps illustrate the point. Document any event you have carried out. Think of five direct consequences or issues that resulted from this event. For each of the five consequences, think of two things that might, did, or will happen because of a direct consequence. Each of these two effects will have their own ripple effect. This continues outward as far as you wish to take it. There is no end.

Now imagine millions of people making decisions and acting on something constantly and what this cause and effect might look like if you went through the same exercise for each event. The magnitude of the effect is unimaginable. Welcome to the Universe. This is the way life works.

Maybe now you have a better appreciation of being told how important it is to choose wisely and base your actions on truth. Whether you do a positive act or a negative act, the ripple effect will set itself in motion. More often than not, positive acts cause good reactions and negative acts cause bad reactions.

This process can also be used to trace events backwards to find where or how they may have originated. Take any situation in the Universe, and look back at events that directly preceded the situation. Then look back again at a second layer of events preceding those. If you had the documentation to rely on, you would actually be able to go back to the beginning of the Universe. Now let's complicate this a little more by throwing into the mix actions that are not based on truth; falsehoods and lies that are starting the chain of cause and effect. Just for fun, mix in a little emotion and drama and there you have it. A Universe in chaos.

We are all suffering because of the current financial crisis. Very few of you had any direct actions that created the situation, yet you are impacted just as much, if not more, than those directly responsible. The consequences of this bad behavior impact everyone because of the ripple effect and because we are all connected. Bad behavior moves both you and the Universe in a direction away from Source. We all have a duty to represent Source conscientiously.

If ever we want to achieve an ideal Utopian-like society, everyone has to do their part. Right decisions. Right actions. Guided by and founded in truth. Know who you are, and follow your path of purpose. This is what Source intended. This is what we must do to fix the Universe.

If mankind would follow this path, the reality of the Universe would be ours to create. Can you imagine a Universe free from illness; free from fear; free from poverty; and free from misery? You would not only be free from these things, but also free to live your life as it was meant to be lived, and free to evolve into who you are meant to be.

Back to consequences.

Everything mankind experiences is created by a series of causes and effects. They are a direct consequence of the choices you make and the actions you take. Are you starting to see how important freedom of choice and actions based on truth is?

You create the state of the Universe based on your thoughts, choices and actions. It really is very basic when you think about it. Source made life easy for us. All we had to do was the right thing. But as Eve exercised her free will to choose the "forbidden fruit," we too often base our choices on falsehood, drama, or emotion.

One of the fatal flaws in human existence is that we are desirous. We cling to wealth, comfort, pleasure, and self-indulgence. We are ignorant of the truth that the desire for the things we seek is the very basis of our suffering.

Once greed fills your mind, you become ignorant of the truth and base your choices and actions on falsehoods. What did I tell you about keeping your mind clear and pure?

Once your mind becomes ignorant of the truth, it thinks wrong thoughts, it loses focus on reality, and it dictates actions that are delusional. Ego takes over and ego knows no truth. It becomes a delusional existence with little or no accountability for consequences.

It is this thought process that causes you grief, pain, and agony. Once you can again bring yourself back to a state of pure thought, you realize that all you really need in life is to follow your path of purpose. That makes everything right and results in happiness and fulfillment.

Don't you wonder why people who exhibit bad behavior for personal motive and greed don't ever worry about being caught? Nor do they seem to be concerned about consequences. They don't think about these things because they are lost in a delusional state of being. Falsehoods become truth. Desire becomes reality. It is a state of confusion. Unfortunately their actions cause much pain and suffering for all those around them.

The good news about the ripple effect and the rules of cause and effect is that they can also be used to rid the Universe of everything that is bad. Imagine that!

You simply need to start making the right decisions, and start taking the right actions, and know that they are right because they are based on truth and nothing else. Along the way, take the time to know who you are and follow your path of purpose. Each right act will have positive consequences that others will react to. Soon, the problems in the Universe will begin to disappear and all mankind will start becoming what Source intended. Life is difficult only because you make it so by desiring satisfaction based on falsehoods. You free yourself from this by following the appropriate rules of behavior.

Where and when did mankind ever get the notion that they are not accountable for their actions? You are accountable not only for the actions you take, but also for all of the rippling consequences that result from those actions. You are accountable for the event, and its cause and effect.

It is delusional thought that teaches you that you can get away with not being held accountable for your actions. Remember that the consequences of your actions not only affect you, but impact the entire Universe and all mankind. Everything reacts to your actions.

All activities in your life should be done with only one intention in mind; fulfillment of your purpose. With that in mind, you need to rid yourself of anything and everything that gets in the way of that destiny. Look inside yourself and get naked. Take off all the clothes that you should not be wearing. Get yourself in a state of clear, pure, and honest thought. Empty yourself and let the Universe fill you. Only then can you start moving forward in a positive manner.

One of the most common reasons for people participating in bad behavior is the falsehood that they must have material things to make themselves happy; money being the primary culprit. They rationalize that anything they do to get it is okay, because they must have it and need it immediately. If there is any one falsehood that people use to define themselves; it is money.

If you follow the process I have defined up to this point, you will find that life is satisfying regardless of financial wealth. You also need to learn that everything you pursue in life is a journey. It never needs to be had immediately nor can it be had immediately without doing the wrong thing.

**Parable of Glenn**
**"The Coin Toss"**

It was a bright sunny morning and I decided to take a walk and enjoy the flowers and the warm sun. As I was walking, I thought a lot about the life I had. My health was good. I drove an old car that ran very well. I lived in a pretty house that was a bit small. And, I had a wife I loved very much. As I rounded the corner, a strange looking man in a suit suddenly appeared in front of me. "Good morning" he said with a smile. I replied "good morning." "This is your lucky day" the stranger said as he reached in his pocket and took out a coin. "I will give you this coin to flip and if it lands on heads you get a nice shiny brand new car. However, if it lands on tails your life will end here and now without any pain or suffering. Would you like to flip the coin?" I finally understood why ever since I was a little boy I carried a two headed coin in my pocket. I said "sure I will flip the coin." He gave it to me and I quickly switched the coin for the one in my pocket. I flipped the coin high in the air and it landed heads up. Poof like magic there was a new shiny car in front of me. The stranger asked if I was willing a take a second chance for a new large house. Of course I said "Yes" and once again threw the coin into the air. Heads again and a new house at the end of the street appeared with my name on the front door. "You are a lucky man" the stranger said. This time the stranger picked up the coin which made me a little nervous for fear that he would catch me cheating. He didn't really look at the coin and asked me if I wanted to try one more time for a million dollars, only this time he would flip the coin. Once again I said, "Yes let's toss the coin one more time." He flipped the coin high into the air and as it was cascading down he said, "This time tails wins and heads you perish."

**MORAL:** You only fool yourself when your journey contains shortcuts and deceptions.

Before we leave the chapter on consequences, I need to talk about one more thing. You know that right actions get positive results and actions based on falsehoods get negative results. Sometimes right actions result in negative consequence because the person seeing the action has a mind that is not pure. They do not see the action for what it is. They cannot see truth. This is what happens when you allow your mind to become impure and delusional. I raise this point to stress the fact of how important it is to rid your mind of non-rational thought. It is as equally important as doing the right thing. Here is an example of what I am talking about.

Bob and Ann have been married for some time and have a good marriage. They are both good people and always try to do the right thing. Recently, Ann has allowed her mind to be poisoned with jealousy. Jealousy is a falsehood that will cause the mind to act irrational and illogical. It prevents you from seeing the truth. One day, Bob met an old female friend that helped him in life when he was going through difficult times. She was a good friend and he had not seen her in years. After catching up with conversation he gave her a hug and a kiss on the cheek to once again thank her for being there for him. As he was doing this, Ann had started to enter the room, but stopped short and watched. Bob never knew she was there. All she saw through her jealous and delusional mind was her husband having intimate relations with another woman. A complete misinterpretation and falsehood. She was so angry that she went storming out of the room and jumped into her car determined to get away from her terrible husband. As she sped off in her car blinded with rage, she runs a red light and hits and kills a woman crossing the street. The woman was pregnant and the news of losing both his wife and unborn child caused the dead woman's husband to commit suicide. The brother of the man who committed suicide was so distraught over the event that he started drinking, which caused his marriage to end in divorce.

All of this happened because the consequence of an innocent good act was misinterpreted by a mind poisoned with delusion. Can you see how important it is to not only do the right thing, but to have a clear and pure mind so that you can see truth when it presents itself? If Ann were rational she would have simply entered the room and asked what was going on. After a brief explanation of the situation, perhaps all three of them could have gotten to know each other better and none of the consequences that followed Ann's irrational response would have ever happened.

This is also a good lesson in the importance of self-discipline and control. All of the people's behaviors that followed the event triggering their reactions was a choice they were free to make. If any person along the chain of events controlled their emotion and acted appropriately, the negative ripple would have stopped. It's all about choices.

Let's take a moment to see what we know up to this point.

You are Source.

You are a spiritual being with a thinking mind.

You are not your body.

You are energy.

You have the power to choose your actions in life.

Your actions need to be right and always based on truth.

Once you know who you are and your purpose, you know your path.

Life is a series of choices, actions, and consequences.

You need to be accountable for your actions.

Consequences have far-reaching effects.

Glenn's
Thoughts

The purpose of this chapter is to show you how important you are to mankind and the Universe. Everything you think, everything you say, and everything you do starts a chain of events impacting all of mankind and the Universe. Whether it is "positive" or "negative"; "right" or "wrong"; "good" or "bad"; the chain of events begins. Because of this, it is so important that you make the right decisions and take the right actions always based on truth.

Be accountable for your thoughts. Be accountable for your words. Be accountable for your actions. And, most of all be accountable for the consequences they cause. I promise you that for every negative situation you experience, it was preceded by an incorrect decision or action by either yourself or someone else. Since we are all connected, any decision or action by you or anyone else, impacts everyone and everything.

Every action you take determines the next event in your life, and how you react to the next event determines the next and so on. The cause and effect of your actions is a never ending chain of consequences. Think before you act and make sure it is based on truth.

America's reaction to events that occurred on September 11, 2001 is an excellent example of consequences. Did we react appropriately? Did we do the right thing? Did we act on fact and truth? Did we react on emotion, rage or revenge? I pose these questions to you so you can ponder them and ask yourself how much of the situation occurring today in our country is a consequence of our reaction to September 11, 2001. It's always about the choices we make, and the truth, or lack thereof, behind those choices.

# Chapter 7:    Contribution

"Aim above morality. Be not simply good; be good for something."

Henry David Thoreau

The Universe provides you with many resources. It provides air that you breathe; water that you drink; food that you eat; and beauty that appeases your senses. The Universe is abundant; however, you are encouraged to make better choices when it comes to using its energy and natural resources. The Universe needs your attention and care, just as your fellow man does. Be eco-conscious.

You have both a duty and an obligation to give back; to contribute. Think of it as payment of a debt. You owe it. The Universe provides a service to you and you have been accepting its gifts with open arms. The Universe allows you to exist. The Universe contains everything you need. The Universe is your life line. You cannot afford to take the Universe for granted.

It's time for you to settle your debt with the Universe. You are being called upon for an expression of gratitude for the privileges and gifts you have been graciously accepting. Life gives unto life.

"You reap what you sow" applies to both your fellow man and to the Universe you inhabit. Whenever possible, you need to help your fellow man and help your Universe.

There are many ways to contribute.

When it comes to the Universe, you need to be energy wise and efficient. Participate in recycling programs. Buy recycled products. Conserve water use. Think solar power. We need to stop burning fossil fuels. Global warming is a real threat.

Be sure to keep the soil in your environment fertilized and healthy. Plant and grow things; especially, those things natural to the native environment.

Keep the environment around you clean and free from liter. The next time you pass a piece of litter, bend over, pick it up, and dispose of it properly. It's good exercise!

Throughout your existence, you need to be committed to give back in order to balance what you consume. When you eat all the sweets in the cookie jar, you fill it again; right?

When it comes to your fellow man, the best contribution is to help them become self-sufficient and self-supporting. Be an enabler of positive contribution. Give encouragement whenever possible. Remind people of their value and how important they are in the Universe. Educate and teach! No doubt you have heard the adage, "Give a man a fish and he eats for a day. Teach a man to fish and he eats for a lifetime." It is part of your natural human spirit to be kind and loving to others.

There is an illness that runs rampant in society. It goes by the name of "entitlement." People exist who get angry and upset because others have more than they do. They have an expectation that they should have everything they want because they deserve it.

These people are the antithesis of the concept of contribution. They are lazy. They do not believe that they have to sacrifice, or work, or earn the things they want. They believe they should have it because they are entitled. These people have lost their way in life; they define who they are by their material belongings. They consume energy from everything and everyone around them. They take without contribution. These are people who need to discover who they really are and need to find their path of purpose. Otherwise, they are destined to misery.

Understand that everything you need is provided to you by the Universe. These things do not come to you without a price. Protect these things so they will always be here for you. After all, you will be here forever.

One more thing I feel compelled to say. When I go places to get things, I refuse to use the drive-through lanes. I park my car, turn off the engine, and walk inside to get what I need. The exercise is good for my body and the Universe needs less exhaust fumes. Please join me in helping to keep the air that we breathe fresh and clean. Imagine the positive ripple effect that will result.

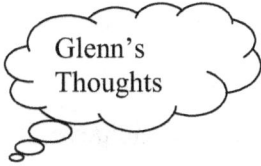

Your value to the community is determined by how your thoughts, words, and actions promote the good of others in the Universe. Only promoting your own good is not contribution.

Along the path we take to fulfill our goal of being who we are is also an obligation to contribute to others and to the Universe. The Universe provides much for us, but we also need to give back to assure what it provides will always be there. We depend on the resources provided by the Universe for our survival. Protect those assets. Do your part to care for the Universe and to nourish the abundance it offers us.

Our greatest personal contribution to mankind is to follow our true path and to fulfill our destiny of becoming who we are. This contribution includes doing the right things based on truth. Whenever an individual fails to achieve these goals, all mankind is impacted in a negative way. Think of mankind as a team that can only win and achieve its positive outcomes when each member of the team accomplishes his or her goal. We all need to do our part. When one fails, the entire team suffers. We are all important!

Because we all need to realize and follow our true path in life, I think it is in our best interest to assure some basic rights to all individuals. I believe that all individuals have a right to eat when they are hungry, and have a right to be treated when they are ill, and most importantly, have a right to be educated when they seek knowledge. For mankind to succeed, we cannot afford to have people who are hungry; or people who are not well; or people who are not educated. We as a society pay a much greater price to have people in these conditions, than it would cost to feed, treat, and educate those who need it.

# Chapter 8:    Healing

"Healing may not be so much about getting better, as about letting go of everything that isn't you; all of the expectations, all of the beliefs, and becoming who you are."

Rachel Naomi Remem

I have never been sick for even a single moment in my life. My body on the other hand is sick quite often, but that's okay, because I am not my body! To fully appreciate this chapter, you need to accept that you are not your body. You are a spiritual being comprised of energy. Everything is energy!

We discussed keeping your non-physical (spirit and mind) in a state of well-being. Doing the right thing and keeping your actions based on truth is what keeps the spirit and mind healthy and well. When you allow falsehoods into your mind, the mind becomes ill with delusion. Your thought process becomes disturbed; your thinking becomes illogical, and your actions will be based on non-truth. You enter a delusional state of being which is the basis of illness in the spirit and mind.

Illness of the spirit and mind happens when you allow falsehoods and drama to be the basis of your actions. You do however have the power to rid yourself of those things by simply choosing to do so. You choose to allow them into your life and you can just as easily choose to make them disappear. Disease of the spirit and mind is one of choice. Do not choose to allow falsehoods to enter your mind. Base all of your thoughts, choices, and actions on truth and you will understand what it means to be free. This will assure that you stay in a state of well being.

The body is a bit more complicated and challenging because it is physical in nature. Physical things are subject to disease and decay. From my perspective, there are three causes of illness to the physical body:

1. Trauma;
2. Genetic Defect; and
3. Negative Energy.

**Trauma.** If you fall down a flight of stairs and break your leg, you have suffered physical trauma and the body is broken. The body is damaged and has changed from what it was before the fall. It will cause you pain and suffering as a result of trauma.

**Genetic Defect.** When it comes to buying new cars, there is something called the "lemon law." If your car does not work the way it was intended to because of construction defect, you may be entitled to a different car. Unfortunately, the body through which you incarnate has no such warranty. Sometimes the body does not work the way it was intended to due to genetic defect. This causes illness, and for the most part, you will have to learn to live with the consequences. There are certainly things you can do to help yourself, and we will cover some of those things later in this chapter.

**Negative Energy.** This is the basis of most physical illness and is a cause that is 100% in your control. Aside from trauma and genetic defect, I believe that all physical illness is a manifestation of negative energy. It starts with allowing energy disturbances and blockages into your body. You have access to unlimited energy. It is all around you; it is inside of you; it is you! You are energy. Negative, stagnant, and stale energy causes bad things to happen to the body. That is why movement and exercise are healthy for the body. Movement allows positive energy to flow freely through the body displacing negative energy. Negative energy damages the body, while positive energy heals the body. The best access to energy is through circular movement.

In order for the body to be in a state of well-being, energy must flow through it properly. Any disturbances in the body flow of energy causes a state of illness in the energy. Eventually, the state of illness in the energy becomes negative, and will manifest itself as illness or disease in the physical body.

Healing needs to occur in the energy source **before** it manifests in the physical body. Keeping your energy positive is a matter of ridding yourself of all negative thoughts, actions and drama. It also means ridding yourself of negative people. Having a clear and pure mind is not only important for decisions and actions, but equally important to keep your body healthy.

> Bad thoughts create negative energy which causes physical illness.
>
> Good thoughts create positive energy which heals the body.

It is very important to know yourself and to pay attention to yourself. The key to healing is to apply treatment **before** the illness manifests in the physical body. It is much more difficult to treat once the manifestation has occurred. Your body was designed to heal itself through free flowing, positive energy.

Let's review!

Source provided you with a spirit and a mind that were in perfect health; however, this is not the case when it comes to your body. Your body can be damaged as a result of trauma or genetic defect. You are in control of the negative energy part of the equation. Most disease that impacts your body is caused by you. When the energy in your spirit, mind, and body are balanced and in harmony, energy flows freely and your body is as healthy as it can be. Imbalance occurs in the spirit because of falsehoods and ignorance.

That is completely in your control! Imbalance occurs in the mind because of negative thoughts and drama. That too is completely in your control! These imbalances result in disrupting or blocking the flow of energy so it stagnates and turns into negative energy. Energy was meant to flow freely. Eventually this negative energy creates a physical state of disease. Negative energy is energy that is trapped in the body without movement. This is what causes the state of disease.

Think of a stream of water that is flowing freely in its natural environment. The flowing water is so clean and fresh that you can drink from it. When something blocks the flow of the water, the water stagnates and starts to collect debris. It eventually turns dark with bacteria and disease, and starts to attract negative things like mosquitoes. When the blockage is removed and the water once again begins to flow, it cleanses itself and returns to its pristine, drinkable, healthy condition.

To rid yourself of physical disease, you must restore balance and harmony between the spirit, mind, and body.

The body follows the state of being in the spirit and mind. The body is not smart like the spirit and mind because it is not you. Balance and harmony restores the flow of energy, once again making it positive. This process washes away the trapped negative energy. To rid yourself of physical illness, you must make healing a daily priority. You need to be able to look inside yourself and find the source of potential negative energy before it manifests into physical illness or disease.

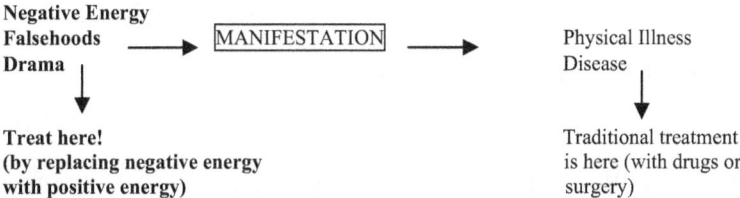

**Negative Energy**
**Falsehoods** → MANIFESTATION → Physical Illness
**Drama** ↓                              Disease ↓

**Treat here!**                          Traditional treatment
**(by replacing negative energy**        is here (with drugs or
**with positive energy)**                surgery)

A body not in a state of well-being is a body out of balance and out of communication with the spirit and mind. It gets out of communication because of trauma, genetic defect, or negative energy. Some causes of negative energy include, drug and alcohol use, poor nourishment, lack of motion, and of course, negative thoughts. With the exception of trauma and genetic defect, all physical illness is a result of behaviors that you are free to choose. Physical illness is most often caused by your thoughts, your actions, and the negative energy you carry inside of you. The energy you carry is also a matter of choice. Rid yourself of negative energy. Fill yourself with positive energy, and you will be well!

I discussed earlier in the book the importance of keeping your thoughts pure, clear, and positive. Now you can further understand how that helps keep your body healthy. Negative thoughts become negative energy which results in physical illness by blocking the flow of positive energy.

All living things have the natural ability to heal themselves. When energy is blocked, low, or negative, it can be replenished with fresh flowing positive energy. You can take positive energy from the Universe, or even from another person. It is all around you. You will find that it is very healthy and feels good to be around people with positive energy, and very unhealthy to be around people with negative energy. Positive energy is healing energy, and helps put balance and harmony back in your state of being.

Healing energy can be transferred directly from the Universe or from one person to another. Some people can heal others with their positive energy, and other people can make you ill with their negative energy. You decide who you want to be around.

Your own state of mind is also a contributing factor. If you do not want to get well, trust me, you won't. As with everything in life, it always comes back to your thoughts and the choices you make. Some people may even manifest illness because they need a reason to prevent themselves from doing something. People choose to use the power of the mind to hurt themselves because they rationalize that it is better than dealing with the truth. The power works equally well; positive or negative. Why ever allow yourself to use it in a negative manner? Again, it's all about choices.

Another secondary cause of physical illness is lack of fresh air and incorrect breathing. This is another reason to take care of your Universe; since it produces the air that you breathe. Meditation is a good practice for learning proper breathing. Meditation teaches you to breathe deeply in through your nose and to exhale completely out through your mouth. It is concentrated breathing that results in cleansing your spirit, mind, and body. I never knew how deeply one could breathe until I practiced this. People tend to inhale and exhale in a very shallow manner in everyday life. You will be amazed at what it feels like to inhale until your lungs are completely full and then exhale until your lungs are completely empty. It is a cleansing experience, and the practice quiets the mind. A quiet mind is a good way of staying connected to Source.

Throughout this book you have been told the importance of keeping balance and harmony with yourself, with your Universe, and with Source. When you add to that the essence and energy of life, you are beginning the journey of evolving into Source. You will have clarity, you will have healing, and you will have inner peace. You will know the truth. You, and only you, have the power to choose this journey of well being. When all people achieve this state, and the Universe is filled with positive energy, all life and existence will be as Source intended; free from illness.

So, what do you know so far about healing?

You have the natural ability to heal yourself and to others through good positive energy. You keep your spirit and mind healthy by keeping it free from falsehoods, drama, and negative thoughts. Your body gets sick from trauma, genetic defect, or negative energy that manifests into physical illness. Keeping your energy flow moving and positive heals the body. Treat your illness at the energy stage before physical manifestation. As always, it's a matter of right choices, right actions, truth, and now, positive energy.

Remember that we are all connected and share energy with one another as well as with the Universe. People with positive energy heal both the Universe and those around them. People with negative energy harm both the Universe and those around them. It's your choice to decide who to be around.

Source intended a Universe filled with people free from illness. This only happens when there is positive energy, positive thoughts, and right behavior, all based on truth. All mankind must work together to promote a consciousness and circulation of positive energy. We must all contribute positive energy and we must all be open to receive positive energy. We can do it. I know we can. It all starts with you. Focusing on the life within you, and the one intended for you, will help you accomplish your evolution into Source.

It is critical to be aware of and treat illness at the energy stage. Traditional medicine treats physical illness once it manifests in the body. It is then most commonly treated with pharmaceuticals or with surgery. This methodology treats your illness, not you. My philosophy is to identify illness at its earliest point and understand what is causing the negative energy so you can rid yourself of it. This all takes place prior to physical manifestation. This practice allows you to prevent illness rather than to treat illness after the fact. In order to be successful with this identification process, you need to be in close touch with yourself. You accomplish that by knowing who you are and having a pure and clear thinking mind.

Understand that most physical illness is created by you. It doesn't just happen. There are some who believe that physical illness may be carried over from one incarnation to another. In either case, it needs to be handled the same way. Whether created by you or by the evolutionary process, you still use positive energy as your method of healing.

All illness, with the exception of trauma and genetic defect, is a result of you making yourself ill by not properly following your path to Source. Your deviations cause negative energy to get stuck in your body. Energy can only remain stuck for so long before it manifests into physical illness.

Once you become physically ill, you will make matters worse by focusing on the illness; or by worrying about the illness; or by complaining about the illness; or by getting angry over the fact that you are ill. All of these reactions create more negative energy which serves to prolong your illness. You need to remember to stay in control rather than have illness control you. Control your thoughts, control your actions, and most of all choose positive energy. Filling yourself with positive energy during challenging times will rid you of your illness very rapidly. It's all about balance and harmony and positive thought. Trust me, it works! Reaching your ultimate goal of having your spirit, mind, and body in perfect harmony with Source will render your body disease free forever.

Haven't you always wondered why two people can catch the same virus at the same time and one will be sick for weeks while the other is fine in a matter of days? Yet another with the same exposure may not get sick at all. The differences are all determined by the positive or negative energy these individuals possess. If you are a negative person and agonize over your illness and complain about your illness, you will be sick for a long time. On the other hand, if you are a person with positive thoughts who thinks this is not a big deal, and that you will be fine tomorrow, guess what, you will be. Finally, if you are that other person who always has positive thoughts, and always has positive energy, and always lives in a state of balance and harmony, you will rarely get sick. You protect yourself with positive energy and a positive state of being.

A great example of this philosophy can be demonstrated through hypnosis. For those who do not understand, hypnosis is nothing more than a state of intensified focus by the mind. All random thoughts disappear and your mind is free to concentrate wholly on the thought planted in it by another person. In other words, you accept what you are told 100% free from any doubt. Under hypnosis, you can tell a person that they are getting very cold and the body actually starts to shiver. Goosebumps form on the skin. The body is cold to the touch and body temperature drops. This is an example of physical manifestations taking place because the mind completely accepts the thought it holds. It is a convincing demonstration of the power of the mind. The body takes orders from the mind. What more can I say, accept, and it will be.

Traditional medicine can never be successful in treating the illness of spiritual ignorance. If that is the source of your illness, you have a problem, no matter what doctors do. They will not be able to help you. Only you can help yourself, through identification of the negative energy within you and fixing your thought process. Also, when it comes to traditional medicine, remember that the Universe was the first physician and healer. The pharmacy of medicine grows all around us. Stay natural with remedies whenever possible. I believe that the Universe has provided us with a natural remedy for any illness we may get; we need to get better at understanding our surroundings.

When you are not capable of healing yourself because your belief system is troubled, and you have not yet understood these concepts and practices, you will have to follow the path of traditional medicine. An appropriate treatment plan rendered by a good doctor will help your body feel better.

I have a theory when it comes to traditional medicine. Doctors for the most part treat illness; they do not treat people. They will take the body's temperature, blood pressure and pulse rate, and make a diagnosis by comparing those numbers to medical standards. The problem with this is that because of the continuous process of evolution, not all people are the same. Therefore the standard of good health for one may not be the standard of good health for another. Yet all patients are deemed healthy or unhealthy on the basis of where they fall within the same standard. I find this concerning. When medicine tries to force everyone to fit the same standard, it conflicts with natural evolution. Traditional medicine is a challenge for people who are more evolved than the current standard used by the medical community.

I am especially concerned when it comes to young children who don't act like everyone else. Too many children are on drugs today for being too hyperactive, or for not paying attention as much as they should, or for acting out more than someone thinks they should. Before you let someone tell you that your child has an illness and needs medication, take the time to determine if you have a child who is more evolved than others, one who should not be held to the standards considered normal. If they are advanced beings, they are not ill. Simply different, in a good way. Help them to find their place and path rather than force them to be like everybody else. Being who you are is not an illness.

Young children are naturally open to receiving positive energy, and allowing it to flow freely through their innocent spirit, mind, and body. Children easily recognize and distinguish positive energy from negative energy. You can see it in their eyes. Unfortunately, they are often led away from Source through exposure to negative conditioning. Allow your children to forever keep the great ability they have to see whatever their mind creates.

Illness and disease is almost always attributed to a misalignment of energy. Keeping your thoughts and actions positive will attract positive energy both from others and from the Universe. It is a natural law of attraction to bring balance back to any misaligned energy. A healthy mind creates a healthy body. Think about it!

A negative lifestyle is the main contributor to being ill. Falsehoods, incorrect choices, lack of good judgment, and even lack of good company all contribute to a state of being out of balance. All of this is entirely in your control. It is your power to choose. You determine your state of well being through an appropriate thinking process. If you allow it to become inappropriate, you allow negative energy to enter your life. Choose a life of free flowing positive energy!

Heal the spirit by acknowledging that it is Source. Heal the mind by keeping it balanced with pure thought and truth. Heal the body with positive energy and by bringing back the balance and harmony between spirit, mind, and body.

Pretend for moment that you do not have a body and you only exist in your spirit and mind state. Your thoughts and your consciousness is all you have. Now draw positive energy and positive thoughts in through your spirit and mind and create the body you want. Think healthy body. Think strong body. Think energy and vitality. Think positive and it will be!

Let the life force of positive energy enter you through your spirit, through your mind, and through your thoughts. Note that the energy stops dead in its tracks when it runs into something negative. Remove those negative blockages and choose to be healthy!

Follow the right laws of living and keep negative thoughts, negative people, and negative energy away from you. Do not allow these things to harm you. They can only hurt you if you let them. Be nice to those who are filled with negative thoughts, but acknowledge who they are, and keep them at a distance.

Another good source of positive energy is the sun. There is nothing better for the body than to be outside when the sun is shining and warm. The sun is one of the best sources of positive energy. Don't hide from it. Allow it to reach out and find your body. Stay safe by enjoying it in moderate doses.

I have noticed an interesting connection in the Universe between troubled times and epidemic illness. The "Thirty

Year War" was fought in Europe in the 1600s. At that same time there was an epidemic of Typhus among the military. This outbreak became known as the "war fever." Then in approximately 1803, Napoleon sent an army of 33,000 to take back French landholdings in North America. Yellow Fever killed 29,000 of those soldiers. In 1862, the American Civil War was being fought; along with a Malaria epidemic.

In more recent times, we saw one of the deadliest outbreaks of influenza. In 1918-1919, right at the end of World War I. It was estimated that this flu epidemic killed between 20-50 million people. In 1928-1929, during the "Great Depression," we saw yet another flu epidemic as well as pneumonia. In 1970, Africa was ravaged from war, and there was much poverty, prostitution and drug use. Coincidentally, this was the start of the AIDS epidemic. Finally, in 1994, Rwanda was in military chaos and an epidemic of Cholera followed the plight of the people into Goma, Zaire.

I don't want to jump to any conclusions, but it seems that when mankind fails to follow the appropriate rules of life, the Universe steps in and imposes its own form of self-discipline. War has never been the right behavior for settling our differences or for obtaining peace.

A nation's negative energy causes nationwide physical illness. A nation plagued with negative thoughts and negative actions has a "ripple effect" of negative consequences resulting in epidemic physical illness. A collective consciousness of negative energy has the power to destroy just as strongly as a collective consciousness of positive energy can save and heal all mankind and the Universe. This is why it is so important for each and every one of you to rid yourself of negative energy and start the flow of positive consequences.

Use the power of choice that you have been given to choose being healthy. Base your life on truth. Always do the right thing. Always keep your thoughts positive and surround yourself with positive energy. Cure any illness you may have at the energy source before it becomes a physical manifestation. You accomplish this by filling your life with positive thoughts and positive energy. Choose good health and be healed. It's always your choice!

I believe we live in a society pre-conditioned to be ill. From the time we are very young we are told; "Don't play in the dirt, you'll get sick"; "If you go out with wet hair, you'll catch a cold"; "If you go out barefoot, you'll get sick"; "If you step in a puddle, you'll catch a cold." Then, as we age there is the constant bombardment of "At this age you may get this illness." So, I have to think, are people really at risk to get prostate cancer at the age of 50, or do we create the cancer when we turn 50 because we accept that it will happen? Talk about negative conditioning! Since the power of the mind is responsible for most physical illness, why aren't we constantly told that you can't get sick!

There is also much evidence today that the more you are exposed to as a child, the more your body activates its natural immunities, and the less you will be sick as you grow older. Let your children get dirty, play in the rain, run around barefoot, and most of all, constantly tell them that they cannot be sick. Never doubt the power of making your children comfortable with their natural state of being. Let's start conditioning our young ones to be healthy and free from illness.

The true secret to healing and being well is to fill yourself with positive energy. It is all around you. It is inside of you. It is everywhere. And, it is yours for the taking. A Universe of wellness has been placed at your fingertips for you to grab as much as you want. It's free! But remember that sometimes you must pay the greatest price for that which is free. To be filled with positive energy, you must first rid yourself of drama, falsehood, and incorrect thoughts, all of which cause negative energy.

Your spirit does not know illness; it only knows what you teach it. Your body has been pre-coded to be what it is. If you allow it to have its way, you have given up your power of free will. You need to accept that wellness comes from a positive state of mind, a mind that thinks and acts only on truth, and a mind that understands who your are and why you are here. Making these thoughts the foundation of the life you live, will forever keep you healthy and well.

Of course you are always going to have to deal with the physical illness attributed to trauma and genetic defect, but you can also recover more quickly from those when you experience life as it was meant to be. When all else fails, traditional medicine is there to help your body. Some day, the healthcare system will make a commitment to keeping people well rather than treating the sick.

Also understand that when it comes to chemical pharmaceuticals, whenever possible, turn back to Mother Nature for a more natural and safe healing experience. You can take traditional medicines for your aches and pains and expose yourself to the side effects, or you can try natural approaches that are all around you. Rather than mask your pain with drugs; make it disappear by eating right and thinking right. The Universe has provided us with natural cures for every illness we may encounter. We need to find them, understand them, and use them.

With all that said, there is no better healer than positive energy and a positive state of mind!

# Chapter 9:    The illusion of time

"I have realized that the past and future are real illusions,
that they exist in the present, which is what there is and all
there is."

Alan Watts

"They say that time changes things, but you actually have
to change them yourself."

Andy Warhol

From my perspective, there is no such thing as "time" in spiritual reality. Spirit time is really a series of states or changes; much like causes and consequences. You experience these series of states regardless of time. For each state you experience, you choose whether to experience it quickly or slowly. You control time in this manner.

There is only one reality; the eternal present. Time is like being born and dying at the same moment. You are always in the present! There is no past; there is no future. There is only the present. Eternal life belongs to those you live in the present. Recollections of experiences, perceptions and thoughts are all memory and memory is a present experience. You always do the remembering in the present.

You are reading this book in the present; at this very moment. When you remember reading this book; your memory will be in the present, at the very moment you remember. If you are contemplating reading this book someday; your contemplation is in the present, at the very moment you contemplate. Everything you think or do whether in reference to past, present or future is always done at the present moment. The present is all that exists.

You live in the present. You think of "past events" in the present. You think of "future events" in the present. You are always in the present! However, thought is so cunning and cleaver, that it distorts this concept for its own convenience. Don't let it fool you. The present is the time that is associated with events perceived directly, not as a recollection or as a speculation.

People tend to focus a lot of attention on the subject of time. We continue to react to things long after they occur. We worry a lot about things that have not yet occurred. We often think "we do not have enough time" to do something. We wish "we had more time." We complain that time moves "too slow" or "too fast." We obsess over time.

If you allow it, the concept of time will drive you delusional. Don't waste your present moment on things that have passed or on things that have not yet occurred. Similar to truth, the present is what it is. You are always in it.

Whether you perceive things as past, present or future, your perception can only occur in the present. You are in the present when you remember something that has passed. And, you are in the present when you contemplate something that has not yet occurred. I know it's a difficult concept; but only the present exists.

My definition of time is **the occurrence of an event**. Time is a series of events that is defined by the order of the events. Time is the moment or point at which something occurs. Events do not occur "in time"; the events themselves are time. Rather than think about "I do not have enough time to live," consider, "The way I live is time." That places the concept of time back under your control because you always choose how you live. You cannot choose "time."

The real issue in life is that things don't get done because you choose not to do them; or you choose to do other things instead. People spend lots of time doing things they don't need to do and neglect things that are really important. This is not a time issue, it is a choice issue. You choose what to do and when to do it...or not. At any given moment, you should be doing whatever it is you are supposed to be doing. In philosophy, the question asked is not, What is the best use of my time right now? but rather, What is the best use of my life right now? This is how you should always be thinking.

I like to look at it this way:

When I wake up in the morning, I do not want to have any leftover thoughts from previous moments. Nor do I want to have any anticipation of next moments. I want to wake up in the present with a clear mind ready to fully experience what is happening at that very moment. The present moment is all there is. Give it your complete attention. I'm certain you have heard the phrase, "there is no time like the present."

Albert Einstein talked about the perception of time flowing from past to present to future as a distortion of reality. Einstein goes on to say that the distinction between past, present and future is only an illusion. In his theory of relativity he states that two people can <u>observe</u> a single event at two different times. The further you are away from the event, the later in time you <u>perceive</u> it; however, the event is actually occurring at the same instant in time. Note the key terms "observe" and "perceive" are what create the illusion of the mind. From a scientific perspective, Einstein explains that this occurs because time is dependent on space; the time it takes for light to travel through space.

Before I finish my reference to Einstein, I need to quote something he said that describes the illusion of time as being nothing more than the mind's perception. It makes a good point with that special sense of humor so unique to him.

"Put your hand on a hot stove for a minute, and it seems like an hour. Sit with a pretty girl for an hour, and it seems like a minute. That's relativity."

The perception of time really depends on what you are doing. When you are unhappy and suffering, you tend to focus on time in a dreadful manner. A minute of pain seems like forever. However, when you are happy and enjoying yourself, you suddenly forget about time like it never existed. I don't need to explain the message here.

Change in life is perceived by comparing two events. When one is different than the other, we can perceive that something has changed. Right at this moment you should start to find it interesting that what I just said sounds more like causes and consequences rather than a theory of time. I hope so!

Memory only exists because of the ability to recall. The act of recall can only happen in the present. The event being recalled happened at the present moment it occurred. You remember it in the present moment. Everything you think and do is in the present moment. The memory of the event only exists because you choose to recall it. It all happens in the present; the original event, the memory, the recall of the event. However, since the present is a series of events, things change. Time doesn't change things; new events change things.

Time is typically measured by a beginning and an end. I have told you that you are eternal. Eternity is without beginning or end; it just exists. It is always in the present moment. Therefore, you cannot define your existence by time. Define it by events; the choices you make. Your present moment is a consequence of your last present moment and your next present moment will be a consequence of your current present moment. It isn't time that changes; it is consequences that change. You control time by the choices you make and by the actions you take.

Time does not affect your choices, or actions, or accountabilities. If you do something wrong, time does not fix it. It doesn't go away because of time. It doesn't get better because of time. It happened; nothing can change that. What you can do is simply make a new choice, perform a new event, and create a new series of consequences based on a right action. The wrong event is past, forget about it, get over it, and move on with a right event.

Based on my definition of time, your choices and actions are what determine next moments. Time becomes defined by the power of your free will. Every action you take in the present moment determines what will happen in the next present moment. You create and define time through your actions and the consequences that result. Your behavior sets the clock in motion and you adjust the clock by making choices. Likewise, you can regard the present state of the Universe as the effect of its past and the cause of its future.

I must continue to stress how important it is to make right choices based on truth to you, to mankind, and to the Universe!

One of the biggest mistakes you can make in your life is to waste your present moment with negative thoughts about past events. If something negative happened to you, don't keep reliving it in your new present moments. It's over; erase it from your memory. Equally, don't waste your present moment with concern about what may or may not happen in future events. The only thing that determines future is your current behavior, since those actions become the consequences of your next moment. If you choose to be concerned about what has not yet happened, than you are creating a negative present moment for yourself.

Mark Twain said, "I am an old man and have known a great many troubles but most of them never happened."

"What you are is what you have been,
And what you will be, is what you do
NOW."

The Buddha

This is probably the most difficult chapter in the book. You need to try to understand because in most cases, the illusion of time has negative impact on your state of well being.

I'd like for you to think of time only as a "reference point of convenience." In your everyday physical life, you need reference points in order to do things. You wake up at a reference point in time; you go to work at a reference point in time; you meet someone for dinner at a reference point in time; the movie you want to see starts at a reference point in time, etc. This makes life convenient from a physical linear perspective. It's needed to be functional in your physical existence.

From a spirit and mind perspective, time does not exist, nor is it needed. This is where we get into trouble with the concept of time. People try to incorporate linear time, or reference points, into their true self; spirit and mind. Once you do this, you prevent yourself from living in the present moment. This creates a problem for the spirit and mind because it only knows the present. That is all that exists.

To prevent this from happening, you need to think of your existence as events occurring rather than time passing. All events occur in the present moment, and are consequences of previous events and will create consequences of next events. Think of time as a series of events that are always occurring in the present. Why is this important?

Once you start interpreting events as time, you stop defining existence as past, present and future. Since there really is no past or future, you begin to use your present to experience life free from carryover from the past and free from concern about the future. This thought process reinforces living in the present moment. When you consider time passing rather than events occurring, you make it difficult to live in the present.

Events occur, then they are over, and the next event occurs. Each event causes the next event; no different than the choices you make since the act of choosing is also an event. When you need to make a choice, you can't make it yesterday (because it's over) and you can't make it tomorrow (because tomorrow comes only when it is the next present.) You can only make your choices in the current present moment. Likewise, you can only live your life in the current present moment, because that is all that exists.

Forget about past events; stop worrying about future events, and make sure your present moments are full of wonderful events!

# Chapter 10:   The path to freedom

"My journey is my journey, how can you comprehend
That what becomes the truth for me is one I cannot lend
Or even simply give away, because it is of me,
It is of me, and me alone, not him, not her, not thee,
A private part of who I am and what I represent,
Impossible to understand from where your journey's sent."

Yanis Bayada

"A human being is part of a whole, called by us the "Universe," a part limited in time and space. He experiences himself, his thoughts and feelings, as something separated from the rest – a kind of optical delusion of his consciousness. This delusion is a kind of prison for us, restricting us to our personal desires and to affection for a few persons nearest us. Our task must be to free ourselves from this prison by widening our circles of compassion to embrace all living creatures and the whole of nature in its beauty."

Albert Einstein

## Your Path To Freedom

∞ You were created in the image of Source.
∞ You are Source. Source is You.
∞ You have all the capabilities of Source.
∞ You are a spiritual being with a thinking mind.
∞ You are eternal energy.
∞ You are not your body.
∞ Keep your body healthy.
∞ Your greatest power is free will; the ability to choose.
∞ Life is a series of choices, actions, and consequences.
∞ Be responsible for your actions.
∞ Choose wisely. Act right.
∞ Base everything on Truth.
∞ Recognize that You are Truth.
∞ Know who You are and your purpose in life.
∞ Your primary purpose is to evolve into Source.
∞ You have your own path to Source.
∞ Do not let anything or anyone stray You from your path.
∞ Know that right behavior gets right results.
∞ Keep your mind clear and pure.
∞ Rid your thoughts of falsehoods.
∞ Contribute to the Universe and it will give back to You.
∞ You have the power to heal yourself and others.
∞ Live only in the moment.
∞ Accept The Power.

You hold the key to the door to enter yourself and in so doing, you enter Source. Let truth be your guide. Base all choices on truth. Free yourself from impure thought. May we all together complete our spiritual journey!


**Accept what I say.**
**Accept that it is good.**
**Accept that it is right.**
**Accept that it is truth.**
        *Glenn*


"For those who believe, no proof is necessary.
For those who don't believe, no proof is possible."

John and Lyn St. Clair Thomas

© THE POWER by Glenn Wolkoff

"May all beings be happy, content, and fulfilled.

May all beings be healed and whole.

May all have whatever they want and need.

May all be protected from harm, and free from fear.

May all beings enjoy inner peace and ease.

May all be awakened, liberated, and free.

May there be peace in the world, and throughout the entire universe."


Metta Prayer

### The Journey

One day you finally knew
what you had to do, and began,
though the voices around you
kept shouting
their bad advice--
Though the whole house
began to tremble,
And you felt the old tug
at your ankles.
"Mend my life!"
each voice cried.
But you didn't stop.
You knew what you had to do.
Though the wind pried
with its stiff fingers
at the very foundations,
though their melancholy
was terrible.
It was already late
enough, and a wild night,
and the road full of fallen
branches and stones.
But little by little,
as you left their voices behind,
the stars began to burn
through the sheets of clouds,
and there was a new voice
which you slowly
recognized as your own,
that kept you company
as you strode deeper and deeper
into the world,
determined to do
the only thing you could do--
determined to save
the only life you could save.

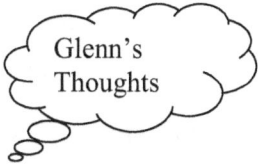

Your path to freedom awaits you. The only thing you need to do is accept it. Everything you could ever need exists in the energy that surrounds you. Through the power of your thought, you can make it real. How you see things is how your life will be.

**You think, therefore, you create!**

Wake up each morning in the present moment with your only thought being empty white space. Let your mind create your day by filling in the space with anything you want to do. Think positive thoughts. Have good intentions. Exercise your power of free will. Most of all, act on truth. If you don't know the truth, then choose your day to be one of finding it.

You find truth by accepting who you are and understanding your path and purpose in life. Following your path will bring you happiness. Along the way, be accountable for your actions because they create consequences that affect not only you, but all mankind and the Universe. Also make sure you give something back to mankind and to the Universe in the form of contribution.

Remember to properly nourish your body and keep your body moving as much as possible. Movement stirs up energy! Enjoy your physical existence, but never forget that you are not your body. Always spend every moment filling yourself with positive energy and emptying yourself of negative energy. The power of positive energy can be used to heal yourself and to heal others. It is the key to wellness. Use it!

You must always live in the present moment. Forget about the issues you create for yourself related to time. Forget your age. There is no yesterday. There is no tomorrow. Live and enjoy life in the present!

Your natural state of being is in a constant relationship with all other beings and with the Universe. We are all connected to everyone and everything through energy.

Your interaction and participation with this energy has great influence on what will be. There is nothing you cannot do. All potential exists in the energy around you. It is waiting for your thought, for your ability to see what needs to be. Thought and energy create the reality of your life.

Understand **The Power** and you will have everything you need in life and you will be happy. As more and more people start embracing "the power," all the right consequences will occur, and all mankind will have everything it needs in life and will be happy. When everyone is following their path in life, the Universe will be everything it was meant to be and will provide for us everything we need. It is then and only then, that all creation will become what it was intended to be; at one with Source!

YOU have the power to make your life what it is meant to be. YOU have the power to make all mankind what it is meant to be. YOU have the power to make the Universe what it is meant to be. It is THE POWER that will allow you to be who you are by following your path of truth. Accept who you are, and the consequences that follow will eternally be the life you always deserved. If you can think it, you can create it!

**...Just another moment in life**

I awoke to a beautiful morning. I could feel the warm rays
of the sun penetrating my being. I could smell the freshness
in the air. The sounds of the Universe were all around me;
children playing, adults laughing, birds singing at the top of
their little lungs, and the quiet rustling of trees in the wind.

I got up and opened all the windows to fill my home with
the positive energy of the Universe. It was invigorating. I
walked outside to pick some fresh fruit and vegetables to
prepare my morning snack. Most everyone grew their own
food.

After a bite to eat, I walked down the street to carry out my
daily purpose in life. Everyone knew their role and
understood who they were. Everyone had everything they
could ever want. Everyone was happy. We all contributed
by being who we are. We all followed our purpose on a
daily basis. If you needed something, it was yours for the
asking. People no longer worked for money and you did

not need money to have anything. In fact, money is a concept long gone and so are the crimes associated with it.

People's decisions and actions support their roles and purpose. It's something like a barter system. Anything I need will be provided by someone fulfilling their role. Likewise, the results of me fulfilling my role are used as needed by anyone else.

Since everyone knows who they are and spends their life following their purpose, all needs are provided through the activities we participate in. Days of the week, months and years are no longer concepts. People are young, spiritual, and wise, and age is no longer something we keep track of.

The Universe is a peaceful place; everyone gets along. There is no longer a need for a legal system. People are also healthy and free from illness. There are a few people who serve their purpose as physicians; treating only those who damage themselves through trauma, and the few with genetic defects. Even genetic defects are becoming less and less common.

The Universe is also a beautiful place with clean air and pristine water. The bright colors of flowers are stunning. Butterflies are everywhere. Every moment is a pleasant moment. Even natural disasters of nature are at a minimum. It must be all that positive energy. The Universe is happy too!

I suddenly had a thought about when the Universe was not this way; when people did not understand their purpose. People made most decisions based on falsehoods. I was busy writing a book at that moment to help people understand the "the power" and "the truth." Enough of this, I think! I am wasting my precious moment with thoughts past; thoughts of hundreds of years ago. A time when my physicality was not what I wanted it to be. I got it right this time. I finally chose a body free from illness, or maybe, I have a body free from illness because I know who I am and what my purpose is.

I live and experience my purpose with every moment; moments filled with joy and positive energy. All my thoughts and actions are always based on the truth of my existence.

My contribution to society is one of being a scholar and a messenger. I created the Wolkoff Foundation of Truth. It's a place where people gather to discuss truth; to discuss their role in fulfilling that truth; and of course, to rid themselves of any falsehoods that may be circulating. A united consciousness is our goal. Truth is our faith. We believe in ourselves and we are free from religious tradition.

I suddenly experience a strong sensation of inner peace as I think about this being a moment in life, a life of being me, and a life of carrying out my contribution to make myself, mankind, and the Universe all that Source intended it to be. There is nothing more powerful than being who you are, and knowing you are Source.

I also contemplate how fortunate I was to have a partner in life that believed in me, encouraged me, and supported me through the process of writing my book. I could not have accomplished it without her. I think of all the past moments in my life spent trying to be like everybody else, only to end up feeling exhausted and empty. Then my wife Jean who I love dearly, manifested before my eyes, and from that moment forward I knew my life had changed. I became me, and knew that the only choice I had was to share what I have come to understand with all those willing to accept it.


∞   Glenn

www.ingramcontent.com/pod-product-compliance
Lightning Source LLC
Chambersburg PA
CBHW031257090426
42742CB00007B/490